P9-DVL-957

paleo

THE REAL FOOD DIET TO RESET YOUR LIFE

REPRINT OF THE TOP SELLER

Elizabeth Marsh

Published by:
Wilkinson Publishing Pty Ltd
ACN 006 042 173
Level 4, 2 Collins St Melbourne,
Victoria, Australia 3000
Ph: +61 3 9654 5446
www.wilkinsonpublishing.com.au

International distribution by Pineapple Media Limited
(www.pineapple-media.com)   ISSN 2203-0832

Copyright © 2015

All rights reserved. No part of this publication may be reproduced, stored in a retrieval system or transmitted in any
form by any means without the prior permission of the copyright owner. Enquiries should be made to the publisher.

Every effort has been made to ensure that this book is free from error or omissions. However, the Publisher, the Author,
the Editor or their respective employees or agents, shall not accept responsibility for injury, loss or damage occasioned
to any person acting or refraining from action as a result of material in this book whether or not such injury, loss or
damage is in any way due to any negligent act or omission, breach of duty or default on the part of the Publisher,
the Author, the Editor, or their respective employees or agents.

The Author, the Publisher, the Editor and their respective employees or agents do not accept any responsibility for the
actions of any person - actions which are related in any way to information contained in this book.

National Library of Australia Cataloguing-in-Publication entry

Creator:	Marsh, Elizabeth Jane, author.
Title:	Paleo : the real food diet to reset your life / Elizabeth Marsh.
ISBN:	9781925265293 (paperback)
Subjects:	Diet therapy--Popular works.
	Nutrition--Popular works.
	Food habits--Popular works.
	Self-care, Health--Popular works.
Dewey Number:	613.2

Cover Design & layout: Tango Media Pty Ltd

Photos by agreement with Rachel Jane Cam.

Every attention and care has been applied to the research, writing and publication of this title, especially in regard to
ingredients, products and services. Reactions may vary from person to person in addition to the variation of availability
and quality of natural and processed foods by region and time. Wilkinson Publishing is not legally responsible for any
negative reaction experienced based on the contents of this book and it is always recommended to consult with your
regular health care provider before making any dietary or lifestyle changes.

PRIMAL
JUNCTION

Contents

FOREWORD

I think we can all agree that food is medicine or food is poison depending on what we choose to put on the end of our fork, spoon or chopsticks —or if you are living the caveman way, what you eat with your fingers.

Never before in history has there been so much talk about what we should or shouldn't eat. Unfortunately the messages are so confusing and every day another claim is made, often distorted by the media to suit their demographics or to keep their advertisers happy. Thankfully the Paleo diet is a practical voice that has risen above the noise in the last decade or two, thanks to the amazing work of passionate and brilliant minds such as Boyd Eaton, Loren Cordain and Nora Gedgaudas, to name a few, who have shone a bright light on what can only be called a common sense and evolutionary science based approach to our optimal eating and health plan.

I myself have been following a Paleo lifestyle for the last 3 years; my own transformation has been nothing short of astounding and I am still constantly learning what is best for my body.

The fact that we now have the global culinary pantry open to us with the abundance of spices, herbs, seafood, meats, fruits and veggies like never before means that we now have the ability to create an astonishing array of healthy meals for ourselves which is literally endless. I have never viewed Paleo as restrictive but instead, utterly indulgent with the choices I now have to play with. I am positive that once you embrace this way of life—as this is what Paleo is all about, a new lifestyle—that you will never turn back, as the energy you will have will be unlike anything before.

Lizzy outlines the dos and don'ts and whys and hows very simply in the following pages and I am sure you will love cooking the delicious recipes that are part of the Primal Junction cookbook... Bon appétite and keep cooking and eating with love and laughter.

Pete Evans
www.thepaleoway.com

INTRODUCTION

Paleo is an opportunity for me to combine my ideas around nutrition, health and lifestyle with the goal to educate and inspire you to live a life you love. After studying in the fields of medicine and exercise science, I became frustrated with the symptom-based and pharmaceutical approach to illness and disease and wanted to learn more about achieving optimal health and athletic performance from the angle of illness prevention. I want to share my knowledge with others so that we can all access our full potential as human beings and live a life of purpose, vitality and fun.

Before my own drastic lifestyle change, I thought I was really healthy. I was following the nutritional guidelines and eating large servings of whole grains, fruits and low-fat foods. I was heavily involved with regular endurance exercise while training for a half Ironman triathlon and was training hard in an attempt to reduce body

fat and still be able to eat the foods that I was supposed to. I became frustrated with fluctuations in body weight and was finding that little injuries were constantly popping up, as well as muscle tightness, fatigue and an overall exhaustion. My times weren't improving and I found it increasingly difficult to keep my eyes open at university lectures. The constant energy crashes and recurring sicknesses meant that I could never be consistent with my training. Although I still thought I was 'healthy,' I knew that something had to change, and fast.

My journey started with an abrupt 30-day self-experiment to completely remove potentially inflammatory and reactive foods from my diet and re-set my digestive system, allowing for repair and regeneration. This was also an opportunity for me to start to learn how to listen to my body and question how it felt in response to a range of food types. I realised that I had eaten many of these foods for so long that I could no longer recognise how they were impacting my health. I reduced my endurance-training load and avoided all processed foods. I began filling my plate with large salads, clean protein and piles of vegetables.

After this experience, I have never looked back. I felt more alive and in tune with my body than ever. Over the 30-day period, I lost 4-5 kilograms (9-11 pounds) of body fat, slept more soundly, had boundless energy throughout the day, clearer skin and an overall enthusiasm and zest for life. I also had a LOT of questions.

Over the last three years, I have explored and researched the Paleo approach and have established a nutrition and lifestyle consulting business, Primal Junction, to share my love of real food with others. I hope that this book will provide you with the tips, tricks, recipes and inspiration to live a life that you love fuelled on real-food. Most of all, I hope that I can encourage you to question the accepted nutritional and health guidelines and take control of your own life by asking questions, experimenting and standing for your health from this moment forward!

WHAT IS PALEO?

The Paleo diet refers to the diet consumed by our ancestors starting some 2.5 million years ago and ending with the start of the agricultural revolution about 10,000 years ago. During this Palaeolithic era, humans lived in small tribes and hunted and gathered their food. Although there were variations depending on location, environment and climate, research shows that these diverse primitive diets consisted mostly of small and large game, fish, vegetables, tubers, fruits, and nuts. Lacking were the grains and legumes, not to mention refined sugars and oils, as seen in modern diets.

With the invention of agriculture, communities were able to start producing larger volumes of food, leading to the industrial revolution and the exploration of refined oils and production of sugar. Along with the influx of these highly refined foods came the onslaught of 'diseases of the Modern Age' such as cardiovascular disease, diabetes, cancer, high blood pressure and obesity. Today, these diseases are affluent in all Western communities and the situation doesn't appear to be improving.

In the Palaeolithic era, food was a necessity and research demonstrates that we did not always have enough of it. Today, what to cook for dinner is one of the most troubling and confusing questions, with an infinite number of answers provided by professionals, online sources, books and nutritional bodies. With unlimited access to processed and refined foods it can be difficult for many to question the modern nutritional guidelines and marketing of industrial food products and get back to basic, real food from small, sustainable community sources.

Contrary to popular belief that early humans lived brutal and dangerous lives with short life expectancies, our early relatives were in fact lean, fit and strong with similar aerobic fitness, body composition and blood pressure values to modern-day trained athletes. Life expectancy values that are commonly used to debate this way of life are in fact skewed by infant mortality rates and early death caused by trauma and injury instead of illness and disease. Even in modern times, there are societies and tribes that are still nourishing themselves by hunting and gathering, with no access to processed food or modern medicine. For example, members of the Hunza tribe from the mountain peaks in the Himalayas frequently live to the age of 130 or greater, and at these ages, still live vibrant, active and high quality lives.

By reconnecting with real food and being conscious about illness prevention, we can re-define what it is to be a human in the modern world. With access to both nourishing and healthful foods, and conventional medical research you can be a lean, physically fit and powerful human being with a zest for life that will extend into old age.

In summary, the Paleo diet is about eating foods that we are genetically designed to eat and that have made up our natural diets for over 2 million years, while avoiding processed and refined foods that have been introduced much more recently. In general, this way of eating avoids processed foods, refined sugar, commercial dairy products, grains and refined oils. Instead, we pile our plates high with high quality and diverse meats, poultry and seafood, lots of vegetables, nuts, seeds, fruits, eggs and high quality saturated fats like coconut oil.

THE MODERN CAVEMAN

Many readers associate the Paleo diet with the carnivorous, harsh and un-hygienic lives of our cave-dwelling ancestors. At first mention of the world 'Paleo', long-haired cavemen equipped with spears and loincloths immediately come to mind. However, the Paleo lifestyle is not about trying to re-enact human life as it was 2.5 million years ago. It's about exploring a real-food and holistic approach to life without the processed and refined foods of the modern world that can be linked to marked increases in disease. It is also about supporting your local communities and knowing the individuals who provide and supply your food. It's about voting with your dollar to promote ethical and sustainable business practice.

Living a Paleo or Primal life is all-encompassing. It's holistic. It's about eating what we're genetically able to process and moving your body in ways that we are designed to move. For our ancestors, movement involved actions like squatting, throwing, hanging, swinging, climbing, pulling, pushing, jumping and lifting. To reach optimal health in the modern world, we need to re-define what it means to be human, reconnect with our natural movement patterns and fuel our bodies with natural foods.

GET HEALTHY, LEAN AND STRONG

The Paleo lifestyle is a way of removing refined, industrial and poor quality foods and adding more nutrient dense and "real" foods in their place. After a lifetime of processed dairy products, chemicals, sugars, refined foods and poor quality ingredients, many people aren't tuned in to how these foods are really making them feel. Without realising that dietary toxins may be the culprit, many of us have unfortunately accepted red-flag symptoms as "normal life". These warning signs may include bloating, body fat accumulation, digestive problems, skin conditions, allergies, chronic pain, irritability, poor quality sleep, fluctuating energy levels, a lack of motivation, depression and/or loss of vitality and passion in life.

By removing reactive and inflammatory foods, the Paleo approach focuses on nutrient dense and whole foods that are easily digested, heal the gut and contribute to muscle growth, fat loss and achieving optimal health. The most exciting part is that the Paleo diet does not require calorie counting or diet foods and is based on eating foods that are recognised by the body with a low level of immune response and inflammation for the majority of the population. After adjusting to a higher fat and more satiating protocol, it is possible to achieve hormonal balance, maintain muscle mass and feel good!

Achieving a long-term, sustainable and healthy relationship with food is about discovering what works for your body, lifestyle and budget. The Paleo diet can be tweaked to suit resistance training, moderate endurance exercise and individual body composition and therapeutic goals.

NOT JUST ANOTHER "DIET"

With the constant turnover of the latest diet trends, new diet books hitting the market and more and more online accounts that are sharing the latest food trend, it's no surprise that many are skeptical about this seemingly new diet that is gaining popularity and making its mark in media and research. In fact, the Paleo diet doesn't include any mind-blowing, new information at all. It's a re-connection with our heritage, traditions and a more simple and holistic approach to nutrition and lifestyle. It seems quite obvious when you consider it, that modern foods that are packaged, preserved or sweetened shouldn't be selected as a preference over foods that are hunted, gathered and grown.

Did every one of our ancestors eat the same foods? Are we aiming to replicate the caveman diet? Of course not! Research by Dr. Weston A. Price studied 14 cultures in detail and found that there were many traditional diets. Some ate no plants, some ate a lot. Some ate raw dairy, others did not. Depending on your individual genetic heritage, you might find that your digestive system is more suited to some food groups over others. For example, if your ancestors were Northern European, there would have been less fresh fruits, raw vegetables and no rice, beans or corn. Cultures that were closer to the equator may have eaten more rice and sweeter fruits. This doesn't mean that you can only eat the foods that appeared in your history, but it does provide

a way to assess your individual food choices in pursuit of optimal health.

Eating Paleo is a template. The information presented is designed to inspire you to *question* the accepted nutritional and exercise guidelines that constantly bombard us from the health industry. The best way to know if something works for you is to try it for yourself. Be consistent, experiment, listen to your body and provide it with the opportunity to 'reset'.

This section will address some of the underlying physiological changes that occur throughout our day to day activities, and also how different foods will make us feel depending on how they are broken down and utilised by the body. By understanding some of the physiological processes, it is often easier to embrace changes to your lifestyle and make the first steps towards cleaning out your pantry!

INFLAMMATION

Inflammation is one of the most important areas to address when wanting to lose body-fat, improve performance or boost your health. Inflammation is not only directly related to the foods that we eat, but also to our hormones, stress levels, type of exercise and lifestyle. Although we generally think of it as a negative reaction to an injury or illness, inflammation is a natural response by the body as a way to protect itself from infection, injuries and intruders. For example, acute inflammation is the redness, swelling and heat that occurs when you cut your finger and is a critical stage in the repair process. Inflammation can become a little less helpful when things go wrong and the body starts to illicit an immune response much more often than it needs to (or chronically), resulting in issues like acne, fatigue, allergies, poor gut health, ulcers, rheumatoid arthritis, asthma, inflammatory bowel disease and more.

Systemic inflammation occurs when chronic inflammation moves beyond the tissues and into the lining of blood vessels and organs. This type of inflammation infiltrates the whole body and places it in an activated immune response state that circulates the blood stream. Long-term systemic inflammation has been shown to wreak havoc on our health and immunity, increasing the risk of developing many modern diseases such as insulin resistance, diabetes, high blood pressure, cardiovascular disease, obesity, neurological conditions and digestive ailments like irritable bowel syndrome (IBS).

As our lives become busier and busier, lifestyle factors that may increase inflammation are on the rise. For many of us, inflammatory foods, busy jobs, high stress, chronic endurance exercise, coffee addictions and processed diets all contribute to the "inflammatory bucket" and it is becoming increasingly important to focus on reducing our level of inflammation to combat this survival mode and allow us to live a big life without the increased risk of disease and burnout.

There are many lifestyle factors that result in an inflammatory response, but not as many that can reverse this state. One of the main influencers on the level of inflammation (and one of the only things we have total control over!) is our diet. Foods can either contribute to our inflammatory response by eliciting an immune response in the body, or help to reduce inflammation by

Inflammation – the silent illness

One of the main issues with systemic inflammation is that it's a silent condition – we may not know that we have it, and the indicators can present themselves as a range of different signs and symptoms that vary from person to person. So how do you know if you're inflamed?

Here's a brief checklist that should give you a little indication.

- ✔ I eat grains
- ✔ I eat processed dairy products
- ✔ I am overweight
- ✔ I carry extra body fat around my abdomen (stomach)
- ✔ I eat processed foods
- ✔ I drink alcohol
- ✔ I eat refined sugar
- ✔ I'm constantly exercising
- ✔ I'm often stressed

This doesn't include the long list of ailments, signs and symptoms that are indicators too. Inflammation can be responsible for acne, illnesses, osteoporosis, joint pain, fatigue, depression, asthma, migraines, chronic pain and much, much more.

providing us with maximal nutrition and minimal reaction. One of the main benefits of the Paleo diet is that the majority of these inflammatory foods are avoided, giving our immune system a chance to rest, re-set and repair.

IMMUNE RESPONSE

Our level of inflammation is somewhat con-trolled by our immune system. Designed to fight 'intruders' and protect the body from bacteria, parasites, viruses and fungi, this complex system will react and attack visitors that are identified as 'non-self.' The easiest entry point for most of these bad guys is straight into our diges-tive system via the mouth. If we are constantly eating foods that our body doesn't recognise, like refined sugars, chemicals and inflammatory foods like gluten-containing grains and legumes, an immune response is generated to fight and pro-tect. For many people, the body is in a constant state of fighting and reactivity, leading to compro-mised immunity. When a serious virus or stressful event presents itself, this baseline inflammation and activation means that the body is over worked and unable to maintain optimal health.

ACID/ALKALINE BALANCE

Food is so much more that just 'healthy' and 'unhealthy.' Above and beyond the immune and inflammatory responses to foods, it may be important to also understand that the acid/base content of foods could have an overall impact on your health. The human body's top priority is to maintain balance (or homeostasis). When we eat foods that are acid-forming (the average Western diet is slightly acidic), the kidneys are involved with registering this change and the body will buffer to bring the pH levels back to normal. Over time, this

acid load on the kidneys can cause problems such as bone and muscle loss with aging, and calcium and other mineral deficiencies.

ACID-PRODUCING FOODS	ALKALINE-PRODUCING FOODS	NEUTRAL FOODS
Meats Fish Grains Legumes Processed dairy products Salt	Fruits Vegetables	Most fats

Source: Cordain, L. *The Paleo Diet*, John Wiley & Sons, Inc. 2011

Note: we need both acidic and alkaline foods to achieve balance. When most people remove the 'filler' foods like grains, bread and dairy products from their diet and focus on eating high quality proteins and fats, they sometimes make the mis-take of not re-filling their plate with alkaline and neutral foods like fats, vegetables and some fruit.

FOODS TO AVOID

SUGAR
Refined and added sugar is omitted from the Paleo diet for a number of reasons. Not only

have we developed processed and refined sugars that far exceed the sweetness found in nature, we have surrounded ourselves with this highly addictive and nutrient-void product.

In the Palaeolithic era, sugar was an extremely rare find. Our ancestors loved honey and were prepared to fight bees to get their hands on it. Other than the occasional beehive, refined carbohydrates were non-existent and even the sugars found in fruits were much less intense. Consider the taste of a wild crab-apple compared to a sweet and juicy Pink Lady!

When we did find sugar, our metabolic processes were designed to make the most of it. The high fructose (a specific form of sugar) content in honey meant that we could eat as much as possible without registering the 'full' centres in our brain. In this era, this was part of survival. The rarity of energy dense foods meant that we needed to store as much as possible for later use. Have you ever wondered why you can eat a whole bag of candy or drink a litre of orange juice without getting full? This 'save it for later' mechanism might explain why.

Fructose metabolism bypasses the brain and heads straight to the liver where it can be stored for later use, or is released into the blood stream as free fatty acids. Problems arise when we "find a beehive" all day long, constantly producing free fatty-acids and burning the constant supply of energy in our bloodstream rather than the fat that we have stored. Excess energy in this form is

What about fruit?

Although modern fruits are a *lot* sweeter than those gathered by our ancestors, they are still a real-food in their whole form. Fruit is a living, natural plant. Although containing varied amounts of different types of sugars, fruit also contains fibre, water, vitamins, minerals and phyto-nutrients.

Depending on your body composition goals, excess fruit can also impact us in the same way as regular sugar-feeding throughout the day so just be aware that an apple for afternoon tea may fuel your addiction to the sweet stuff rather than help you break it. A great guideline is to always stick to fruits in their whole form and look for those that contain lower levels of sugar, particularly if you are insulin resistant or wanting to lose body fat. Eating some fats or protein with your fruit will also help to slow the insulin response of your snack or meal. For example, you could have a small handful of nuts or some slices of chicken breast with your afternoon fruit snack.

The table below shows a few examples of the higher and lower total sugar options (not necessarily ranked in order).

LOWER SUGAR FRUITS	HIGHER SUGAR FRUITS
Lemon and lime	All dried fruit
Avocado	Grape
Strawberry	Banana
Papaya	Mango
Grapefruit	Apple
Blueberry	Pineapple
Fresh fig	Pear

Source: Cordain, L, Fruits and Sugars, Sugar content of Fruits, http://thepaleodiet.com/fruits-and-sugars/

stored as body fat. Therefore, rather than blaming dietary saturated fats for our obesity epidemic, it makes more sense to make the connection between a drastic increase in refined sugar intake and the storage of excess energy as body fat.

As well as the reliance on sugar instead of fat for fuel, continual 'sugar hits' throughout the day mean that we need to secrete more of the hormone insulin to regulate blood sugar levels. Over time, excess production of insulin can lead to insulin resistance, and in more severe cases, type 2 diabetes. By reducing our reliance on refined and potent sweeteners, we can control blood sugar with less insulin release and reduce the risk of developing these types of metabolic conditions.

For most of us, cutting sugar out of our diet isn't an easy task. The over-stimulation of our taste buds and pleasure centres means that it is harder and harder to satisfy cravings and almost impossible to appreciate the sweetness of foods like strawberries, carrots or vine-ripened tomatoes. The reward-response from sugar also means that it's highly addictive. When you stop your intake of sugar abruptly, your body suffers withdrawals and this can manifest as headaches, fatigue, crankiness, frustration and poor performance.

After the initial period of suffering, normally around 5-7 days, our taste buds regenerate and the taste of food actually *changes*. You will start to taste the sweetness in fruits and vegetables and your body will not be on the lookout for sugary foods as a mid-afternoon pick-up. Soon, you'll feel fuller for longer as you'll be starting to rely on fats for fuel rather than regular sugar spikes. This also means that your blood sugar will stabilise, you'll have less excess carbohydrate to store as body fat and you'll bounce out of bed in the morning, ready to tackle the day.

SWEETENERS – REAL AND ARTIFICIAL

As more research surfaces and confirms the numerous health conditions and illnesses associated with a high intake of refined sugars, an increasing number of sugar alternative products have become available on the market. Whether a sweet product is marketed as natural, raw, unrefined or calorie-free, sugar is sugar.

Both natural and artificial sweeteners will provide a pleasure-response and fuel our reliance on sweet foods and sugar-fixes without adding any nutritive value to our day. Artificial sweeteners are just that – artificial. They offer no nutritional value and are designed to make us believe that a food is sweet when it's not. The chemical processing of sweeteners like Nutra-Sweet, Equal, Splenda and stevia places them on the no-go list. In general, it's best to remove the majority of sugar (natural or artificial) from the diet and focus on sourcing carbohydrates from whole fruits and vegetables. When you consider the diet of our ancestors, sugar was not something consumed daily, or even weekly!

DON'T BE FOOLED

Sugar is added to many foods on the industrial food chain. Be sure to check the ingredients list of all foods and aim to buy those that don't need an explanation! Sugar is often disguised under many different terms, so we've distinguished some of the best options for you. If you are making the occasional sweet treat, choose these when you can and avoid other 'natural' and all artificial sweeteners as much as possible. Not sure how to use these sweeteners? Check the back of the recipe section for some cleaner sweet treat ideas.

- Dates (whole)
- Fruit (whole)
- Fruit juice
- Raw honey
- Maple syrup
- Molasses

DAIRY PRODUCTS

Most of the time, dairy products fall into the 'avoid' category on the Paleo diet. However there is a huge difference between the dairy products available on your supermarket shelves and those in their natural form. In the Palaeolithic era, dairy products were not included in the diet beyond the mother's milk provided to an infant for fast growth and immunity.

When dairy products are prepared for supermarket shelves, the pasteurisation and homogenisation processes can destroy the nutritious and helpful bacteria, leaving an acid-forming and inflammatory food with not a whole lot of nutritional value. Many individuals are sensitive or even allergic to dairy – often diagnosed as lactose or casein protein intolerance. Even worse, low-fat dairy products are often full of sweeteners and artificial flavourings.

Some followers of the Paleo diet may decide to keep some forms of dairy in their day. This may be because they have a low reactivity or intolerance to products like full-fat, organic yoghurt, grass-fed butter or raw (unpasteurised and unhomogenised) milk. Of all the dairy products, these contain the highest amount of nutrition, healthy fats and helpful bacteria.

WHAT ABOUT CALCIUM?

It is a common belief that dairy products are the only source of calcium in our diet. This is just simply not true. Calcium is important for many cell processes, including muscle contraction when we exercise, and is present in high amounts in green leafy vegetables, seafood, nuts, fruits and vegetables.

The most important consideration, however, is the balance between calcium *excretion* and calcium *absorption*. This is intricately related to the acid-alkaline balance that was discussed earlier. Calcium and other important bone minerals are required to assist with the buffering process when we eat a diet high in acid-forming foods like cheeses, grains, dairy, meat and eggs. Instead of eating more foods high in calcium, we can decrease the amount of calcium that we excrete by consuming more alkaline foods. A Paleo diet high in alkaline vegetables and fruits neutralises the dietary acid caused by meat and seafood and reduces the risk of bone loss and osteoporosis. This balance is particularly important for athletes with a higher utilisation of minerals like potassium and calcium. Load up on fresh fruits and vegetables to promote strong bones, injury prevention and healthy muscle contraction.

REFINED OILS

The Paleo diet incorporates the use of healthy, naturally occurring and minimally processed fats and oils. There are a few important features of oils and fats to consider – their stability, smoke point and how they've been made.

Industrial oils like peanut, 'vegetable', sunflower, corn, canola and rice bran oil have been through a comprehensive refining process to convert seeds and grains into a cheap and highly reactive product. These oils are high in polyunsaturated fatty acids (PUFA) and omega-6 fatty acids – fats that have been shown to promote systemic inflammation and are highly unstable when heated due to a low smoke point.

Contrary to the nutritional guidelines over the last 30-40 years, high-quality saturated fats are in fact the best choice for storing, heating and eating to promote health, satiety and flavour. The connection between saturated fats and heart disease has been shown to be flawed, with research now uncovering many important factors such as fat quality, smoke points and other lifestyle factors like sugar and processed and refined food intake when considering heart disease risk.

Saturated fats, like coconut oil and animal fats are a stable and unreactive source of fatty acids. These fats can withstand higher cooking temperatures and will last a lot longer in your pantry. They do not become rancid easily, and are therefore the best choice for cooking and baking.

The table below summarises the fats and oils to choose for both hot and cold uses, as well as the industrial products to dispose of when you clean out your pantry. Make sure all fat sources are organic, pasture-raised, grass-fed, extra-virgin, cold-pressed and sustainable (check the food quality section for more info).

GRAINS, LEGUMES, NUTS AND SEEDS

Removing grains is one of the biggest changes when people transition to a Paleo diet. This means no more breads, pasta, rice, cereals or

SATURATED – FOR HEATING	UNSATURATED – FOR COLD USE	POOR QUALITY – DISPOSE
Coconut oil	Extra-virgin olive oil	Margarine
Palm oil	Sesame oil	Canola oil
Butter	Macadamia nut oil	Corn oil
Ghee	Walnut oil	Grape seed oil
Meat	Avocado oil	Rice bran oil
Seafood	Flaxseed oil	Rapeseed oil
Animal fats (bacon, tallow, duck fat)	Nuts	Sunflower oil
Full fat dairy	Seeds	Safflower oil
Eggs	Nut and seed butters	Soybean oil

High-quality saturated fats are the best choice for storing, heating and eating to promote health, satiety and flavour.

corn (yes, corn is a grain!). This food group became a staple part of the human diet after the agricultural revolution, just 10,000 or so years ago, and is now recommended as one of our primary sources of carbohydrate. The main reason that grains and legumes are mostly avoided is because they are storehouses of anti nutrients called lectins, a natural defence mechanism for plants that protect them from being eaten! Lectins are low-grade toxins that are extremely hard for us to break down and can cause many inflammatory and gastrointestinal complications, including leaky gut syndrome. This condition can increase the permeability of the gut wall and allow toxins and partially digested food particles into the bloodstream, possibly triggering an immune reaction, inflammation and illness. Not only do they play havoc with our digestion, anti-nutrients can also inhibit our ability to absorb beneficial nutrients like magnesium, calcium, zinc and iron.

Although often touted as a healthy Paleo snack, nuts and seeds also contain high levels of anti-nutrients too, and just like grains and legumes, should be properly prepared prior to consumption. In fact, cashews have higher levels of anti-nutrients than most grains!

To reduce the amount of anti-nutrients (like phytic acids and lectins), these foods should be soaked and rinsed prior to cooking. Optimal soaking times vary, so if you're wanting to include these in your diet then do your research first! In the recipes that follow, most nuts are listed as pre-soaked or "activated" for this reason.

GLUTEN

Gluten is a protein composite found in several types of grains including wheat, rye, spelt and barley. Gluten is named after its glue-like texture and is a sticky protein that gives bread and pasta its elastic properties. The main problem with gluten is the reactivity that it can cause in the body. For individuals that are sensitive to gluten, particularly those who have been diagnosed celiac, gluten is treated in the body like a foreign invader. The immune system will turn on an 'attack' as a protective mechanism, which can lead to digestive discomfort, nutrient malabsorption, anaemia, fatigue and an increased risk of developing diseases like cancer, autoimmune diseases, anaemia, bowel disease, neurological diseases and more. In fact, a review paper in *The New England Journal of Medicine* listed 55 "diseases" that can be caused by eating gluten. There is no benefit to eating this inflammatory protein, and most people will find that they feel better without it in their diet. Often it is difficult to tell whether you react to gluten, as symptoms can be silent or unrecognisable because we are so used to feeling tired and bloated and have accepted this as 'normal' life.

SOY PRODUCTS

The Paleo diet excludes all soy products, both refined and fermented. Soybeans are legumes in their natural, raw state and are in fact poisonous and must be cooked. Similar to other legumes and grains, soybeans are high in phytates that reduce the bioavailability of nutrients.

The main reason to question and remove most soy products completely is related to the way in which they can interfere with estrogen receptors in the body and alter the natural control of this important hormone. Unfortunately soy products and their industrial by-products are present in a large amount of packaged foods and livestock feed. Soy most commonly appears in soybean oil, which is a highly reactive and refined oil high in non-favourable Omega-6 fatty acids that can have a negative impact on health when we over-consume them.

FOODS TO EAT AND WHY

Now to the exciting part! The best thing about the Paleo diet is all the delicious, nutritious and colourful foods that will fill your plate and provide you with the nutrients and energy to bounce out of bed in the morning and live a life that you love.

An important thing to remember when changing your eating habits and consuming a lot less "filler" foods like bread, pasta, rice and cereal, is to make sure that you're eating *enough*. One of the most common errors is to cut out these large food groups without replacing the energy provided by these foods with other sources. For example, if your breakfast normally consists of two pieces of toast with two eggs and a slice of bacon, you may be disappointed and hungry when you remove the bread and don't add anything in its place. In this situation, there are a number of ways to bulk up your plate with nutrient dense foods that will keep you full for longer. Instead of inflammatory and energy dense

toast, pile up your plate with some sweet potato fritters (page 52), vegetables, half a grapefruit, fresh berries or cauliflower 'rice' (page 84).

FATS

Fats are an extremely important part of a healthy diet. Fats contribute to our hormone health, skin health and immunity. The primary sources of fats in the Paleo diet come from animal fats, clarified butter, ghee, fish oils and seafood, avocados, olives, eggs, coconut products and some nuts and seeds.

By consuming healthy fats with each meal, we can teach our bodies to burn fats more efficiently as a fuel when we're walking, cleaning, cooking and at work. This means that we can burn more body fat at low intensities. For some endurance athletes, a higher fat diet will allow them to utilise this energy dense fuel source and preserve their carbohydrate stores for later in a race or when it's needed most.

FAT QUALITY

When we focus on real, whole foods, it is also important to address food quality and to know

Although contrary to the "saturated fat causes heart disease" debate, a meta-analysis compiled by the *Journal of Clinical Nutrition* looked at 21 studies that followed more than 300,000 participants for up to 24 years, tracking saturated fat intake and incidence of heart attack and stroke. They found no significant evidence to conclude that dietary saturated fat intake is linked to an increased risk of coronary heart disease, stroke or cardiovascular disease.

Source: Hartwig, D and M, *It Starts with Food*,
Victory Belt Publishing, 2012.

where our fuel sources are coming from. This includes purchasing foods without health claims and nutrition labels, and voting with our dollar to support local butchers, grocers and farmer's markets. Ideally, we'd be switching over to local, organic, seasonal and well-raised sources, but sometimes this can involve an increase in food costs. There are certain considerations that may have a bigger impact on your health than others, so I'll recommend how to make this transition a little easier and more affordable.

Fats are particularly important when considering food quality, as many of the toxins, pesticides, hormones and chemicals that are used to produce higher volumes of food more cheaply are fat-soluble, meaning that they are 'held' and stored within an animal's fatty tissue. This is also the case for dairy products like butter and ghee – organic and grass-fed sources will contain fewer toxins than commercially available supermarket products. Just like they're held in an animal's fatty tissue, these toxins can be stored and build up in our own tissues too. If you don't have access to grass-fed, organic sources of meat, we recommend that you trim the fat before cooking and eating. With cleaner sources of meat, there's no problem with eating the fatty trim!

Nuts and seeds are another source of fatty acids on the Paleo diet. As with all foods however, we need to make sure that we're eating these nuts in their most natural form. As nuts are high in unsaturated fats, their delicate oils can be damaged easily. It's best to go for raw, organic nuts that are from local sources if possible. Often nuts that are imported can be fumigated or treated. To increase the bioavailability of nuts and to make them more digestible, soaking before use is ideal to remove some of the nutritional inhibitors and toxins.

PROTEIN

Protein is an important macronutrient for recovery, repair, satiety and many chemical processes that take place in the body. Protein is involved with enzyme formation, and is therefore a critical component for processes like digestion, metabolism and DNA repair.

On the Paleo diet, dietary protein sources come from meat (both farmed animals and wild game), seafood and eggs.

PROTEIN QUALITY

As with fats, the *quality* of our protein sources is critical to reaching optimal health. With the goal to prepare and consume foods that are closest to their natural form as possible, it becomes important to address how our protein sources are fed and raised. For example, if a cow that is genetically designed to graze on grass is raised on a grain-based diet, this will impact the quality of the meat, health of the animal and inevitably the health of those who are consuming its meat. Not only does the meat taste better and support a sustainable and more environmentally friendly industry, meat from grass-fed animals has a superior nutrient profile, with more Omega-3 fatty acids, less impact from stress hormones and more micronutrients and vitamins, like vitamin A precursor beta-carotene and vitamin E.

The same goes for eggs. Chickens that are raised on an un-natural diet high in grains, hormones and supplements will produce a lower quality egg than those that are 'pasture raised' and allowed to roam and graze on worms and insects. Many conventional eggs come from chickens that never go outside and are raised in cages to promote mass-production.

The best way to ensure that you are supporting ethical, sustainable and healthy farming practices is to ask! Ask your local butcher about their sources of meat. Find out what chickens are fed, visit farms and request change. If we can all ask more questions and stand for the health of our animals, food and community, we can vote with our dollar to change the way that animals are farmed and our food is treated.

CARBOHYDRATES

Although many believe that the Paleo diet is a low or no-carbohydrate diet, it's possible for most individuals to reach adequate carbohydrate needs through the large amounts of both simple and complex carbohydrates found in real-food. Many current diets or eating plans have created a fear or negative attitude towards carbohydrates and sugars, when in fact they are a critical ingredient for a healthy human diet and were a sought after energy source for our hunter-gatherer ancestors. The problems arise when we consume refined and artificial sweeteners in excess. Healthy carbohydrates, contrary to most nutritional guidelines, are those that are as close to their natural form as possible, easily digestible and full of bio-available nutrients. Carbohydrates are extremely important to provide energy for exercise, important physiological functions and for fuelling important organs like the brain. For all these processes to take place however, the micronutrients, vitamins and minerals involved must also be present in the body. For this reason, when we eat carbohydrates in the form of refined sugar, like in a soft drink, this takes an inflammatory toll on the body rather than providing it with the nutrients and energy required to train hard or live a big life.

Our carbohydrate needs depend on the amount of energy we utilise throughout the day. For example, a person that is sedentary for most of the day will require a lot less fuel than an athlete who is training twice per day. When we eat carbohydrate (no matter what form it's in), our body will use this energy first, preventing us from tapping into the energy dense fat stores that many of us would like to make use of! When we eat too much carbohydrate, excess is easily and efficiently stored as body fat. When we eat too little, particularly for active people, we can feel sluggish, tired, and irritable and may experience plateaus in performance.

There are a range of carbohydrates that all have a different effect on the body and the resulting blood sugar response. On the Paleo diet, our main carbohydrate sources come from dense high-carb vegetables and fruits. The list below includes some of the real-food vegetables that are highest in carbohydrate. For athletes, these foods are great to reach for as part of a post-workout meal to refuel muscle glycogen (stored energy).

As mentioned previously, fruits in their whole form are also a great carbohydrate source on the Paleo diet. To ensure that we

FOOD	CARBOHYDRATES PER 100G
Yam	27g
White potato	22g
Sweet potato	21g
Parsnips	17g
Beetroot	10g
Onion	10g
Carrot	10g
Butternut squash	10g
Spaghetti squash	6g
Pumpkin	5g

Source: Sanfilippo, D, *Practical Paleo*, Victory Belt Publishing, 2012 get all the fibre and nutrients that come with them, blending them or eating them whole is a preference over juicing. Mix up your fruit and vegetables as much as possible to ensure that you have access to a wide range of nutrients, vitamins and minerals.

CARBOHYDRATE QUALITY

When you purchase your weekly fruits and vegetables, a good question to consider is "how close is my food to its natural state?" This includes genetic modification and chemical sprays added to fruits and vegetables. Buy organic produce as much as possible from a local, sustainable and seasonal source. If this is not achievable, local produce is preferred over conventionally grown and genetically modified products. Check your local environmental governing body for information about the most heavily sprayed "dirty dozen" and least contaminated foods. In general, wash all fruit and vegetables really well and peel any conventionally grown produce that you can. Better yet, grow your own food. Lettuce, herbs and green leafy vegetables are a great place to start and will generally grow easily and in small spaces.

THE PALEO TEMPLATE

There is no one diet or eating plan that will suit every individual. Whether you're training for a marathon, working towards better digestive health or fighting an illness or disease, the Paleo diet can be adapted to suit your goals and your lifestyle.

When working with individual clients to address their nutrition, inflammation and body composition goals, I recommend that they experience a 30-day 're-set.' This is a 30-day protocol or challenge that is similar to an elimination diet. The re-set allows your digestive system

to rest and repair while reducing the intake of inflammatory foods allows the immune system to take a break from its reactive state. It encourages us to consume the cleanest foods possible, and experience what life is like without a constant influx of refined foods.

After the 30-day re-set, it is interesting to start adding back in some of the foods that you may want to experiment with, like some forms of dairy, grains or legumes. This protocol allows you to become aware of how these foods make you feel and most people never go back to allergens like wheat, gluten and sugar after discovering how these impact their energy levels, digestion and overall health. Experiment with your own body, meal plans and lifestyle. Find out what makes you bounce out of the bed in the morning and what foods slow you down and make you sluggish.

TOOLS OF THE TRADE

All recipes in this book are easy, fast and delicious ways to fill your plate with nourishing, whole foods and without refined, processed and potentially harmful ingredients. Cooking for the Paleo diet is fun, sometimes challenging and always rewarding. There are endless Paleo recipe sources available both online and in books, and magazines. The more you cook, the more you will learn to substitute certain ingredients and work with a creative flair to turn your old favourites into clean, primal alternatives.

The following gadgets are some of the *extra* tools that will assist you in creating all the recipes provided in the book, and are helpful additions to any Paleo kitchen. No devices on this list are necessary, but are just nice to have!

A powerful blender: A high quality blender is a great tool for liquid recipes like smoothies, soups, nut butters, milk alternatives and drinks.

A food processor: Food processors with a couple of different bowl sizes will be your go-to for dips and marinades, ice-cream alternatives, sweet treats, mashes and puréed vegetables.

An immersion or hand-held stick blender: These are fantastic small devices that you can take with you! They are also the easier option for in-the-pot pureeing and soup-making. This gadget will make Paleo mayonnaise in a matter of seconds.

Slow cooker (crock pot): A slow cooker is particularly valuable in cooler months, when you want to come home to a nourishing, warm and tender meal. Slow cookers can be large enough to make big stews, curries and soups for dinner, with plenty of leftovers!

Pressure cooker: This appliance is fantastic if you want to cook tender meals in less than half the time. By cooking at a high pressure, this large pot will cook sweet potato in less than 10 minutes and a delicious fall-off-the-bone pot roast in about 40 minutes. These are great for those that get home from work and want to pre-pare a slow cooked meal in less than an hour.

Vegetable spiraliser: Vegetable spiralisers are a big hit in our kitchen. They are amazing tools that can turn vegetables into spiralled noodles, a great alternative for pastas. If you'd rather something smaller, a hand-held julienne device will make vegetable 'noodles' out of vegetables like carrots and zucchini too.

Microplane: These fine graters are ideal for fresh ginger and lemon zest, often called for in primal recipes and real-food cooking.

Ice-block moulds: These are handy little tools when you have kids at home, or if you like to have a frozen treat in the freezer over summer. Look for BPA-free plastic moulds and it's best if they have little drinking straws to help with melting pops!

PANTRY GUIDE

At Primal Junction, we recommend that clients kick off their re-set or dietary change with a big clean out of the pantry. If you're taking the step toward a Paleo lifestyle and better health, make the commitment and remove all processed or tempting foods while you make the initial adjustment. Check the nutrition panel of every product and if there's added sugar or nasty chemicals that you don't recognise – throw it away. If it's been in your pantry for longer than 6 months, it probably needs to go.

This will open up so much space for new, clean ingredients and staples. As we want to focus on real-food, you might find that your pantry is a little more spacious than before!

The initial swap from high-preservative and industrial foods to cleaner, organic and higher quality options can sometimes come with a hefty bill. Remember, you don't need all the things on this list at once. If you transition slowly and purchase one or two items with each shop you won't be spending big; without high ticket purchases like cereal, muesli bars and confectionery, you should be able to work these products into your budget. Remember, this is an investment in your health – your reduced medical bills will make up for it in the end!

This is just a brief summary of things you can incorporate into your diet but the options are endless and creativity in the kitchen is your best friend!

OILS AND FATS	IDEAL OPTIONS
Extra virgin olive oil for cold uses	Organic, extra-virgin and cold-pressed
Macadamia nut oil for medium cooking temperatures	
Coconut oil for high heat grilling, frying and baking	
Grass-fed butter for medium cooking and baking	Organic, from grass-fed cows
Ghee or clarified butter	Organic
Nuts and nut butters (peanuts excluded as they are a legume, not a nut!)	Raw, organic and without other ingredients
Coconut cream and coconut milk	Organic with no strange ingredients. Look for BPA free cans and 100% kernel extract.

SAUCES + CONDIMENTS	IDEAL OPTIONS
Coconut aminos: similar to soy-sauce but gluten and wheat free	Organic
Tahini: ground sesame seed paste	Can be hulled or un-hulled
Mustard	Avoid added sugar, corn starch or oils
Pasta sauce	Avoid added sugar, flavourings and preservatives
Passata (tomato puree)	Avoid additives and sugar
Tomato paste	Organic and without preservatives
Apple cider vinegar	Organic or biodynamic
Hot sauce	Avoid added sugar
Pesto	Avoid poor quality oils or make your own

If you're taking the step towards a Paleo lifestyle and better health, make the commitment and remove all processed and tempting foods.

SPICES + SEASONINGS	IDEAL OPTIONS
Moroccan or Cajun seasoning	Sugar and preservative free
Dukka/harissa	
Curry powder	
Ground cinnamon	Look for Ceylon cinnamon
Cumin	Organic and preservative free
Garam masala	
Turmeric	
Paprika	
Nutmeg	
Chilli	Fresh or chilli flakes
Ginger	Grated, fresh ginger is best
Salt: so many varieties! Smoked, seasoned etc	Choose pink Himalayan salt or ground sea salt

ADDED EXTRAS	IDEAL OPTIONS
Coconut flakes	Organic, with no preservatives or additives
Desiccated coconut	
Goji berries: delicious chewy texture	
Cacao powder: high in magnesium	Raw
Cacao nibs: chocolate hit	Raw
Apple puree	Look out for added sugar and preservatives
Probiotics	Sauerkraut, fermented vegetables and kombucha
Stock cubes	Make your own or look for organic without preservatives.
Frozen berries and fruits	Organic

EAT WHOLE FOODS	ELIMINATE PROCESSED FOODS
VEGETABLES	**GRAINS**
The Paleo diet promotes pretty much all types of whole, organic, fresh vegetables. Discover a wide range of local and seasonal veggies to get access to a diverse range of vitamins and micronutrients.	Remove both whole and refined grains like cereals, breads, pasta, rice, wheat, barley, quinoa, millet, buckwheat and corn.
FRUITS	**PROCESSED FOODS**
Aim for lots of different varieties of fruit. Choose lower sugar fruits for a smaller blood sugar response.	Avoid all packaged and processed foods like muesli bars, pastries, protein bars, potato chips, candy, and chocolate bars. Look for hidden preservatives and chemicals.
PROTEINS (MEAT, SEAFOOD, EGGS)	**DAIRY PRODUCTS**
Choose meats from sustainable, grass-fed and organic sources when possible. Choose from a diverse range of meats including wild game, organ meats, and seafood. Look for organic eggs from pasture raised chickens.	Eliminate all processed dairy products including milk, yoghurt, cottage cheese, ice-cream and cheeses. Raw, unprocessed dairy is an option for some individuals.
NUTS AND SEEDS (PROPERLY PREPARED)	**SWEETENERS**
As you start the Paleo diet, nuts can be a great snack option. However, they are easy to over-consume and can slow fat-loss results if this is your goal. Improve the nutrient absorption of your nuts and seeds by soaking them first.	Choose only natural, raw sweeteners in small amounts. This may include raw honey, maple syrup, dates and fruit. Avoid *all* processed and refined sugars including artificial sweeteners. Look for hidden sweeteners in most packaged goods!
FATS AND OILS	**REFINED OILS**
The quality of fats is very important when aiming to reduce the levels of toxins in the diet. Hormones, chemicals and toxins can all be stored in poor quality fats. For cooking, choose saturated fats like coconut oil, animal fats and ghee. For cold or low temperatures, choose nut oils and cold pressed olive oil.	Dispose of refined oils like margarine, sunflower oil, canola (rapeseed) oil, vegetable oil, rice bran oil and any old oils that have been exposed to light and/or high heats. Buy oils in small, dark bottles and keep them in a cool, dark cupboard or in the refrigerator.

Recipes

DRINKS AND SMOOTHIES

Raw protein shake
Skin food green smoothie
Banana cacao bliss
Anti-inflammatory ginger tonic
Hide the greens smoothie
Coconut iced coffee
Infused waters
Espresso nut milk
Spiced carob and nut milk hot chocolate

Raw protein shake

Although processed protein powders can vary in quality with cleaner options now available on the shelves, these refined foods and fine powders can still wreak havoc on the gut. If you want to stick to real-food protein sources, try this raw egg smoothie.

2 raw eggs (add extra egg whites for a bigger protein hit)

1 cup (250ml) coconut milk (or almond milk)

1 tbsp raw cacao

1 frozen banana (100g)

1. Add all ingredients to a blender or food processor.
2. Pulse until well mixed, thick and creamy.

TIP: Top with some raw cacao nibs or ground cinnamon to serve

Raw eggs can seem daunting to some, but as long as you purchase them from a pasture-raised, ethical source, they are a safe and nutrient dense food, rich in high quality fats and protein. Eggs contain a little bit of almost every nutrient we need!

Skin food green smoothie

To me, true beauty is about health, happiness and a passion for life. One of the first places we notice this type of exuberant and energising beauty is in healthy, glowing skin.

This green smoothie is a creamy, delicious 'skin food'. With avocado, peppermint and coconut oil on the ingredients list, this smoothie is jam packed full of fatty acids, antioxidants and vitamins that will promote a healthy glow on the inside and out.

5 large kale (Tuscan cabbage) leaves, de-stemmed

½ avocado

1 lime, peeled

1 green apple, peeled and cored

½ cup (10g) fresh peppermint leaves (or mint)

1 tbsp coconut oil

3 ½ cups (875ml) filtered water

1. Wash all ingredients well.

2. Add all ingredients to your blender and blend on high for 90 seconds, or until smooth and creamy.

3. Serve with ice cubes and slices of fresh lime.

Banana cacao bliss

This recipe is a clean and creamy substitute for chocolate milk. If you have kids in the house this is an after-school treat that will give them a healthy dose of essential fatty acids, magnesium and carbohydrates to keep them satiated and fuelled up until dinner.

4 cups (1 litre) nut milk (page 34)

1 large frozen banana, without peel

3 tbsp raw cacao powder

½ tsp allspice

½ tsp pink Himalayan salt

½ tsp vanilla (or a couple drops of essence)

1. Add all ingredients to a blender or food processor.

2. Pulse until well mixed, thick and creamy.

3. Store in an airtight jug in the refrigerator and shake well before serving.

TIP: If you're currently adding protein powders to your diet, this is a great base to provide fats and carbohydrates for refuelling post-exercise.

Anti-inflammatory ginger tonic

Start your day with a dose of this refreshing tonic full of anti-inflammatory gingerols and alkalising fresh lemon. If you're used to waking up and having coffee on an empty stomach, try some ginger tonic first to reduce acidity and kick-start digestion.

1 lemon, peeled

35g (3 tbsp) chunk of ginger, peeled (adjust depending on the strength you like)

4 cups (1 litre) filtered water

1 tbsp raw honey** (optional)

1. Add the lemon, ginger and water to your blender.

2. Blend on high until smooth (about 90 seconds).

3. If you want a pulp-free drink, pour the mixture through a nut milk bag* into your jug.

*If you don't have a nut milk bag, you can easily use a piece of muslin cloth or don't strain if you don't mind some ginger pulp.

**Honey has great antibacterial and anti-inflammatory properties so add a dash if you want to gently sweeten your tonic or if you're fighting a sore throat or cold.

INGREDIENT SPOTLIGHT

Ginger root is known to contain an abundance of potent anti-inflammatory substances called gingerols. For this reason, ginger is often used as a natural approach to the treatment of arthritis, joint pain and tendinitis and may in fact have a better therapeutic profile and fewer side effects than non-steroidal anti-inflammatory drugs. When we stress our system during endurance exercise, ginger may help to reduce systemic inflammation and inflammation linked to surrounding recurring injuries. Instead of reaching for a processed pharmaceutical option – why not try some of what nature has to offer?

Hide the greens smoothie

This smoothie is a great way to sneak some extra leafy greens into your day without even knowing it! Kale, like other members of the Brassica family, contains health promoting phytochemicals sulforaphane and indole-3-carbinol that appear to protect against a range of cancers such as prostate and breast cancers.

½ cup (85g) natural macadamia nuts

2½ cups (625ml) filtered water

1 cup (130g) frozen raspberries (or another frozen berry)

1 frozen banana

5-6 large kale (Tuscan cabbage) leaves

½ small beetroot, peeled

1. Soak macadamia nuts and water in a blender for 15 – 30 minutes to help soften the nuts.

2. Add the rest of the ingredients and blend on high for 90 seconds or until smooth.

3. Add water as required to reach your desired consistency. Garnish with mint leaves or frozen berries.

Coconut iced coffee

2 shots black espresso coffee, cooled

¼ tsp vanilla extract

½ cup (125ml) cold water (or to taste)

3 tbsp coconut cream

1. Fill a large glass or jar with ice.

2. Add the coffee shots and vanilla. Stir to combine.

3. Add the cold water to desired strength.

4. Top with coconut cream before serving.

Infused water

When transitioning to a Paleo diet, many people don't know what to drink! Our favorite beverage choices are herbal tea, kombucha and these delicious infused waters. You can make them ahead of time and store them in the refrigerator in a large jug, or grab-and-go sized bottles.

Cucumber, mint and lime

lemon and ginger

raspberries and lemon

cinnamon and turmeric

1. Slice, chop or squeeze the above ingredient combos into filtered water. You can adjust the flavour intensity by changing the amount of each ingredient.

2. Allow to infuse for 4-8 hours, and then remove any large chunks if you want to store your water for longer. Consume within 3-4 days.

3. Get creative with your own additions and flavour combos!

TIP: These infused waters look beautiful in a large glass pitcher or water dispenser. For a chilled version, you can also freeze the berries, lime slices or lemon first! You can also use a coconut water base for a sweeter version.

Espresso nut milk

½ cup (75g) 12-hour pre-soaked cashew or macadamia nuts

1¼ cups (310ml) filtered water

2 shots (30ml) high quality organic espresso

1 Medjool date, pitted (optional)

Pinch of Himalayan rock salt

1. Place the soaked nuts and water in a blender and blend on high for 90 seconds, or until smooth and creamy.

2. Add the espresso, salt and date (if using).

3. Blend again, on high, until well combined.

4. Serve chilled.

TIP: Just like other crops, coffee beans can be heavily sprayed and fumigated. Try to source locally grown, organic beans when possible.

Spiced carob + nut milk hot chocolate

This winter warmer is a treat to make at home when it's chilly outside and you have some extra homemade nut milk! Watch out for store-bought nut milks that have a very low concentration of nuts and often added preservatives and sweeteners.

1 cup (250ml) homemade activated almond milk (or another nut milk)

1 tsp fresh ginger, finely grated

1 cinnamon stick, crushed

1 star anise

½ vanilla pod

½ tbsp carob powder

Pinch of turmeric

Pinch of pink Himalayan salt

1. Place the nut milk in a small pot over low heat.

2. Add all other ingredients and stir well.

3. Simmer on low (the milk shouldn't boil) for about 10-15 minutes, until warmed through.

4. Pour the mixture into your mug through a strainer and discard all the spices.

5. Serve warm!

BREAKFASTS

Rhubarb and apple crumble pots
Bacon and onion 'egg-ins'
Raspberry-coconut chia pots
Breakfast crumble
Holy-moly banana pancakes
Clean mean muesli
Chorizo and chilli frittata
Sweet potato fritters
Spicy steam-fried eggs on cauliflower rice

Rhubarb and apple crumble pots

—— SERVES 4 ——

On a Paleo diet, we remove a lot of the 'filler' breakfast foods like toast, cereal and yoghurt. In their place, we often reach for eggs as a staple protein. When we're in a rush or feeling like a lighter breakfast these crumble pots are a great alternative.

FOR THE FRUIT BASE

4 stems fresh rhubarb, leaves removed

400g canned pie apples* (check the ingredients to make sure it's 100% apple)

*If you don't have access to canned apples, make your own stewed apples by slow cooking chopped apple pieces until they soften.

FOR THE CRUMBLE

2 tbsp pepitas (pumpkin seeds)

2 tbsp sunflower seeds

2 tbsp sesame seeds

⅓ cup (40g) raw slivered almonds

⅓ cup (30g) shredded coconut

½ tsp Himalayan pink salt

½ tsp cinnamon

1 tsp chia seeds

¼ cup (25g) goji berries, roughly chopped

raw pistachio nuts, chopped

1. Wash and chop the rhubarb into small chunks. Add to a pot with about 3cm/1 inch of water. Bring to the boil then reduce to a low simmer until the rhubarb chunks start to soften and fall apart (about 15 minutes).

2. Allow the rhubarb to cool while making the crumble topping.

3. Into a dry pan over low heat, add the pepitas and sunflower seeds. Stir constantly as they lightly toast for about 2 minutes.

4. Add the sesame seeds, almonds, coconut, salt and cinnamon. Stir constantly as all ingredients are lightly toasted for another 2 minutes. Avoid high temperatures as this will cause the nut and seed oils to react and turn rancid.

5. Remove the nuts and seeds from the pan and place in a bowl to cool.

6. Once cooled, stir through the chia seeds and chopped goji berries.

7. In the bottom of a bowl or glass, place a layer of apple (about 3cm/1 inch thick).

8. Add a layer of stewed rhubarb of a similar thickness.

9. Top with a layer of crunchy crumble and a sprinkle of chopped pistachios.

TIP: Pre-make the fruit base and store in recycled jars in the fridge. On your way out the door or when you get to work, top with the crunchy crumble and enjoy.

Bacon and onion 'egg-ins'

—— MAKES 12 ——

12 slices of high quality streaky bacon

12 large eggs

4 spring onions (scallions), finely chopped

Smoked paprika

Chives, to serve

1. Preheat a conventional oven to 175°C/350°F.

2. Cut baking paper into 12 7cm x 7cm (3 inches x 3 inches) squares and line a muffin tray with them.

3. Line the sides each muffin cup with a slice of bacon to create a ring. The bacon ring will hold the paper in place. Bake in the oven for 10 minutes or until crisp.

4. Meanwhile, crack eggs into a large jug, add the onion and mix well.

5. Remove the tray from the oven and pour the egg mixture evenly into the 12 bacon baskets. Don't worry if it goes outside of the bacon ring just aim to evenly fill the muffin holes.

6. Dust each egg-in with some paprika.

7. Bake at 175°C/350°F for 25 minutes or until the tops are starting to brown and the egg is cooked through.

8. Sprinkle with chives to garnish.

Store the egg-ins for up to four days in an airtight container in the refrigerator. They are a perfect grab-and-go breakfast or daily snack.

Raspberry-coconut chia pots

1 cup (130g) raspberries, fresh or frozen

1 cup (250ml) coconut cream, chilled (plus extra to serve)

1 tsp pure vanilla extract, or ½ fresh vanilla bean, scraped

¼ cup (40g) chia seeds

4 tbsp coconut flakes

2 tbsp goji berries

pinch of sea salt

¼ cup (30g) fresh blueberries, to serve

¼ cup (30g) pomegranate seeds, to serve

4 mint sprigs, to serve

1. Thaw the raspberries (if frozen) and mash them with a fork into a smooth paste.

2. Add the coconut cream, vanilla, chia seeds, coconut flakes, goji berries and salt and mix well until combined.

3. Allow to set overnight in the fridge. The chia seeds should absorb some of the moisture and form a thick, gel-like consistency.

4. When ready to serve, divide into 4 glass jars or bowls. Top with some coconut cream or coconut yoghurt, fresh berries, pomegranate and mint.

Breakfast crumble

3 Granny Smith apples (350g/12oz), peeled and chopped

2 cups (260g) mixed berries, fresh

2 tsp cinnamon

1 cup (100g) almond meal

½ cup (35g) coconut flakes

½ cup (50g) raw, sliced almonds

3 tbsp ghee, coconut oil or butter, melted

2 tbsp maple syrup (optional)

½ cup (125g) coconut yoghurt (optional, to serve)

1. Preheat the oven to 180°C/350°F.

2. Place the apples and berries into the bottom of a non-metallic baking dish and gently mix together with 1 tsp of the cinnamon.

3. In a medium bowl, mix together the almond meal, coconut flakes, sliced almonds and the remainder of the cinnamon. With your hands, massage your oil of choice and the maple syrup (if using) into the mixture until crumbly.

4. Evenly spread the topping over the fruit base and cover with aluminum foil.

5. Bake for 20 minutes covered, and then remove the foil and bake for another 8-10 minutes uncovered or until golden brown.

6. Serve with a high quality coconut yoghurt.

Holy-moly banana pancakes

1 banana

½ tsp ground cinnamon

½ tbsp almond butter

2 eggs

1 tbsp coconut oil

FOR THE TOPPING

½ cup (65g) frozen strawberries or berries of your choice

1 tsp balsamic vinegar

1. Put the banana, cinnamon, almond butter and eggs in a blender. Blend until well mixed and a little fluffy.

2. Place a large pan over medium heat and add the coconut oil. Once hot, slowly pour the pancake mixture into the pan (about 9cm/3 inches across). When bubbles start to form on the surface, flip the pancakes and cook through the second side.

3. For the topping, defrost the strawberries in the microwave for 30 seconds until soft (you can also do this in a pot if you prefer). Add the balsamic vinegar and mix well using the back of a fork. Topping should be sauce-like.

4. Serve with any toppings that you like!

Here are some creative pancake topping ideas: walnuts, maple bananas, cinnamon, raspberries, coconut flakes, passionfruit or cashew cream.

Clean mean muesli

1 cup (168g) raw almonds

1 cup (140g) natural macadamias

½ cup (60g) raw pistachios

½ cup (80g) raw cashews

2 cups (150g) organic, dried coconut chips (flakes)

½ cup (70g) pepitas (pumpkin seeds)

¼ cup (40g) chia seeds

1 tbsp ground cinnamon

1 tbsp ground fresh ginger

¼ cup (60ml) coconut oil

1. Preheat the oven to 85°C/185°F. Low temperatures will help to avoid damaging the healthy nut oils and create crispier muesli.

2. Roughly chop all the nuts into chunky pieces.

3. Mix all the dry ingredients in a large bowl. Add the coconut oil and mix well.

4. Spread the muesli in a thin layer on a baking paper lined oven tray.

5. Bake for 15 minutes until crispy and starting to brown.

6. Let the muesli cool and store in an airtight container.

TIP: Serve muesli with homemade nut milk or sprinkle on top of smoothies.

Cashew cream

—— MAKES 1.5 CUPS ——

1 cup (160g) raw cashews, pre-soaked

1 cup (250ml) filtered water

1 Medjool date, pitted

1. Place all ingredients in a powerful blender or food processor.

2. Blend on high until the nuts start to form a smooth paste. You may need to use a wooden spoon to stir the mixture occasionally, or even add water to reach the right consistency.

3. Store in an airtight container in the refrigerator for up to 3 days to use as a sweeter side for breakfasts or desserts.

Chorizo and chilli frittata

—— **SERVES 4-6** ——

1 tsp coconut oil

1 high quality chorizo, sliced

1 garlic clove, crushed

½ hot red chilli, de-seeded and roughly chopped

½ white onion, diced

½ red capsicum (pepper), chopped

1 can (400g/14oz) chopped tomatoes

2 tbsp sliced Kalamata olives

8-12 eggs (depending on the size of your dish)

Fresh micro-greens, to serve

Handful of cherry tomatoes, to serve

Salt and pepper

1. Preheat the oven to 175°C/350°F and line a frittata tin with baking paper.

2. In a medium saucepan, heat the oil over a high heat. Add the sliced chorizo and pan fry until crispy and browned. Transfer to a plate and set aside.

3. In the same pan over medium heat add the garlic, chilli and onion and stir until translucent and soft.

4. Reduce to medium heat. Add the capsicum, olives and canned tomatoes and simmer for 15 minutes, stirring occasionally.

5. Into a large bowl, crack the eggs and whisk well.

6. Pour the eggs into the lined tin. Gently spoon the tomato mixture into the centre and use a fork to slowly stir the egg and sauce together using a circular motion. This will create a 'marbled' look when the frittata cooks.

7. Place in the oven for 10 minutes until the eggs start to cook. Remove from the oven and place the chorizo slices on top of the frittata. Put it back in the oven and bake until cooked through (another 5-10 minutes).

8. Garnish with micro-greens, cherry tomatoes and salt and pepper.

This recipe works for individual servings too. Follow the steps as above and spoon the mixture into a muffin tray or small frittata tins, simply adjust the cooking time accordingly.

Sweet potato fritters

1 medium sweet potato
(400g/14oz)

1 egg

1 tsp salt

Ground black pepper, to
taste

1 tsp Moroccan seasoning
(check for hidden sugars)

2 tbsp coconut oil

1. Peel the sweet potato and grate using a food processor or cheese grater.

2. In a large bowl, crack the egg and whisk. Add the sweet potato, salt, pepper and Moroccan seasoning to the egg and mix well.

3. Heat the coconut oil over high heat and add the batter to fit as many fritters as possible in your pan (¼ cup or 3 tbsp at a time).

4. Fry for 2½ minutes on each side. The edges should start to brown and the fritter will hold together when you flip it.

5. When done, remove from the pan and serve warm. Fritters are a great replacement for toast, pancakes or on their own.

TIP: Once cooked, the fritters freeze well in an airtight container or bag. Pop them in the toaster to defrost on the spot!

These fritters are a fantastic transition food when you feel like toast or need something to hold up your eggs! They are delicious served with hard-boiled or poached eggs.

Spicy steam-fried eggs on cauliflower rice

This recipe uses a technique called steam frying. It's an easy, no-flip way to create a perfectly cooked fried egg without having to cross your fingers that the yolk won't break!

1 tsp smoked paprika

½ tsp sesame seeds

1 tsp chilli flakes (optional)

½ tsp salt

1 tsp ghee (or coconut oil)

4 eggs, at room temperature

1-2 tbsp water

1 cup cauliflower rice (page 84)

1. Mix the paprika, sesame seeds, chilli and salt in a small bowl.

2. Use a large fry pan with a glass lid and heat the ghee over high heat. Swirl it around to coat the pan.

3. Reduce to medium heat and gently crack the eggs into the pan. Sprinkle with the spice mix.

4. With the lid in one hand, pour the water into the hot pan and cover immediately.

5. The water will create steam that swirls up and over the eggs, cooking them from the top down.

6. As soon as the yolk becomes white in colour, remove the pan from the heat. The white should be cooked through and the yolk still runny.

7. Serve the eggs on top of salted cauliflower rice.

TIP: Create the flavour that you like by mixing up the seasonings. This recipe is also delicious when the spice blend is substituted for Moroccan or Cajun seasoning, or a pre-made dukkah.

SNACKS

Clean zucchini slice
Rana's Baba Ghanoush
Kale chips
Dijon devilled eggs
Seared sesame tuna spring rolls
Apple chunks with toasted cinnamon-coconut butter
Sweet potato chips
Mama's mayo
Nut-free snack mix

Clean zucchini slice

⅔ cup (150g) bacon (look for one without nitrates or added sugar)

3-4 cups (600g) grated zucchini (about 3 medium sized)

2 small brown onions

8 eggs

1¼ cups (140g) raw almond meal

⅓ cup (75g) macadamia nut oil

1 small red chilli, finely diced

1. Preheat the oven to 175°C/350°F and line a 15 x 30 cm (6 x 12 inches) dish with baking paper.

2. Dice the bacon and fry over high heat until brown and crispy.

3. Meanwhile, wash and grate the zucchini and onions.

4. In a large mixing bowl, whisk the eggs and then stir through the almond meal. Add the zucchini, onion, oil, chilli and pre-cooked bacon and mix well. The mixture should be just pourable.

5. Pour into the lined baking dish and bake for 40 minutes or until cooked through.Leave to cool before slicing into small squares. The slice should last in the refrigerator for 3-4 days and will freeze well too!

Rana's Baba Ghanoush

Thanks to an inspiring member of our Primal Junction community, Rana, for this delicious and easy paleo-friendly dip!

2 medium (450g/1lb) purple (globe) eggplants

1 tbsp macadamia nut oil

1 tsp ground cumin

⅓ cup (75g) hulled tahini

juice from half a lemon

1 garlic clove, chopped

2 tbsp olive oil

½ cup (10g) fresh parsley, chopped

1 tsp Himilayan rock salt

1. Preheat the oven to 190°C/375°F.

2. Chop the stem off the eggplant and slice in half lengthways. Brush with the macadamia nut oil and sprinkle with ground cumin. Roast for about 15 minutes, or until browned. Set aside to cool.

3. Once cooled, use a sharp knife to remove the skin from the eggplant.

4. Add the eggplant flesh, tahini, lemon juice, garlic, olive oil and parsley into the bowl of a food processor and pulse on high until smooth.

5. Serve with lamb, vegetables, salad and veggie sticks!

Kale Chips

When transitioning to a cleaner diet, it is often difficult to find snack foods that hit the spot when you are looking for something salty and crunchy. These kale chips are super easy to make and can be seasoned in lots of different ways to mimic some of the snack foods that we're used to. Kale (also referred to as Tuscan cabbage) is an amazing power food. Per calorie, kale has more iron than beef and more calcium than milk, and is packed full of vitamins A, K and C, and antioxidants with cancer-fighting properties.

1 large bunch (700g/1.5lb) of kale (Tuscan cabbage), washed

2 tbsp (25g) melted coconut oil (or Ghee)

Salt to taste

1. Pre-heat the oven to 175°C/350°F and line a large tray with baking paper.

2. Remove the kale leaves from their fibrous stems with a knife or by tearing them off with your hands. Tear the leaves into bite-sized pieces.

3. In a mixing bowl, add the kale, coconut oil and salt and mix really well with your hands to coat the leaves.

4. Scatter onto the baking paper one layer thick.

5. Bake in the oven for 7-10 minutes, until the kale is still green in colour but crispy and dry. These paper-thin chips can burn very quickly so watch them closely in the last couple of minutes.

6. These will stay crispy in an airtight container for a couple of days.

TIP: Spice up the flavour of your kale chips by adding different spices and seasonings. Here are a few favourites to add to your chips before they go into the oven.

- French onion: ½ tbsp onion powder + 1 tsp garlic powder + 1 tsp salt
- Smoked chilli: ½ tbsp smoked paprika + 1 tsp chilli flakes
- Cheesy: 1 tbsp nutritional yeast + 1 tsp mustard powder
- Anti-inflam: 1 tbsp turmeric + 1 tsp ground ginger
- Spice: 1 tbsp cinnamon + dash of cayenne pepper

Dijon devilled eggs

—— **SERVES 4** ——

These tasty little morsels are a great option for a pre-made quick breakfast or a snack high in protein and good fats. They'd be a great option for guests at brunch.

4 eggs

3 cups (750ml) water

1 tsp baking soda

4 slices (100g) high quality ham off the bone

1 tsp macadamia or coconut oil

1 tbsp Dijon-style mustard

1 tsp apple cider vinegar

Salt and pepper, to taste

1 tbsp paprika

1. Gently place the eggs in the bottom of a saucepan and add the water and baking soda. Make sure the water completely covers the eggs. Baking soda helps to separate the egg from the shell (making it easier to peel) by drawing some of the egg's water content out through the shell into the pot. Older eggs will also peel more easily, so choose eggs that are at least a week old to get dent free devilled egg baskets.

2. Heat the saucepan over high heat and when the water starts to boil, wait one minute before turning off the heat and covering the pot.

3. Leave the eggs for 10 minutes before dunking into ice water to arrest the cooking process.

4. Meanwhile, dice the ham and pan-fry with the oil until brown and crispy. Leave to cool.

5. Peel the eggs and slice in half lengthways. Scoop out the yolks into a separate bowl using a teaspoon.

6. Add the ham, mustard, vinegar, salt and pepper to the yolks and mix well to create a paste.

7. Using a teaspoon, evenly scoop the mustard mixture into the egg-white baskets.

8. Season each devilled egg with some paprika and a little salt.

TIP: For takeaway Dijon devils, press the two egg halves back together and store in an airtight container in the refrigerator.

Sesame Tuna Spring Rolls

250g/9oz tuna steak (yellow fin tuna is great)

⅓ cup (75g) sesame seeds (mixed white and black)

1 tsp black pepper, freshly ground

1 tbsp macadamia nut oil (or coconut oil)

1 small Lebanese cucumber, sliced into strips

1 bunch fresh coriander (cilantro), roughly chopped

1 small red chilli (optional), sliced

1 small carrot, thinly sliced

1 small bunch fresh watercress

8 large cabbage leaves, cut into squares

Edible flowers, to serve

DIPPING SAUCE

½ cup (125ml) tamari (for a soy-free option, use coconut aminos)

1 tbsp fresh ginger, finely grated

2 tsp sesame oil

2 tbsp fresh lime juice

1. To make the dipping sauce, place all ingredients in a small bowl, mix well and set aside.

2. Heat the macacdamia nut oil in a large frying pan over medium–high heat. Cook tuna for 1½ minutes on each side or until cooked to your liking.

3. When cool, slice the tuna into thin strips.

4. Serve spring roll ingredients on a platter with the cabbage leaves and all other filler ingredients for DIY rolls.

TIP: Mix up the DIY ingredients to create all different types of rolls. You can use different coloured cabbage leaves, smoked salmon, avocado, spices and seasonal ingredients like tropical fruits and chutneys.

Apple chunks with toasted cinnamon-coconut butter

Granny smith apples (approx ½ apple per person)

4 cups (300g) organic coconut flakes

½ tsp cinnamon

1. Preheat the oven to 180°C/350°F.

2. On a large baking tray, place a sheet of baking paper. Spread the coconut flakes out evenly on the tray.

3. Place the coconut in the oven and keep an eye on it! The flakes will burn very quickly, so keep mixing them around until evenly browned. Remove from the oven and set aside to cool.

4. Place the coconut flakes in your food processor with the cinnamon.

5. Pulse until the coconut becomes smooth and resembles nut butter. You may need to scrape the sides of your food processor every minute or so.

6. Chop the apples into chunks and serve with the coconut butter.

TIP: You could add all sorts of flavours to this recipe like vanilla or sea salt, or even combine it with some other nut butters too.

Sweet potato chips

—— SERVES 3-4 ——

Orange sweet potatoes are one of the best sources of beta-carotene. As carotenes are fat-soluble, make sure you enjoy them with some healthy fats to get the full benefit of this vitamin A precursor. This recipe pairs the sweet potato with coconut oil to help with nutrient absorption.

2 medium sweet potatoes (about 250g or 9oz each), very finely sliced

2 tbsp coconut oil, melted

salt, to taste

cinnamon (optional)

1. Preheat the oven to 175°C/350°F and line a large tray with baking paper.

2. In a large bowl, combine the sweet potato slices and coconut oil until all sides are lightly coated.

3. Lay the slices in a single layer on the baking paper. If you have extra potatoes, use a second tray or cook two batches.

4. Place in the oven and bake for 10 minutes on each side (watch closely as they burn quickly)

5. To bring out the flavour of the sweet potato, sprinkle with salt and cinnamon to taste. These are best served straight out of the oven!

Mama's mayo

There are lots of Paleo mayonnaise variations that use high quality oils instead of rancid vegetable oils and preservatives that you'll find lurking in supermarket varieties. Although we'd usually recommend an extra virgin, cold-pressed olive oil, this recipe calls for a light flavoured olive oil as we found that other oils were quite overpowering compared to the mayo that we're used to.

1 egg, at room temperature

2 tbsp apple cider vinegar or lemon juice

½ tsp Dijon-style mustard (or dry mustard powder)

½ tsp salt

¼ tsp cayenne pepper (optional)

1¼ cups (310ml) extra light tasting olive oil

1. In the jug/cup of a handheld stick-blender, add the egg, vinegar, mustard, salt, cayenne pepper and 1/4 cup (60ml) of the light olive oil. Process until just combined.

2. Add the olive oil, and blend on low while holding the blender firmly. The oil, egg and mustard will form an emulsion almost immediately and you'll create a thick mayo instantly!

3. Transfer to a recycled jar and store in the refrigerator for up to a week.

Note: if you don't have a handheld blender, you can create the same texture with a food processor by slowly adding the olive oil in a very thin stream as the food processor churns on low power.

TIP: For herbed mayo, stir in a ¼ cup (5g) chopped fresh herbs like dill, coriander or parsley.

Nut-free trail mix

Why go nut free? Although the digestion and nutrition of nuts can be improved by preparing them properly (soaking and activating them), nuts can be high in anti-nutrients like phytic acids. These can play havoc on the digestive system and contribute to problems like leaky gut syndrome and can also prevent us from absorbing nutrients like magnesium, calcium, zinc and iron (page 17). This easy snack will provide you with a hit of nutrients, high quality fats and carbohydrates for that mid-afternoon pick-me-up, without the usual nuts that often make up the bulk of trail mixes.

¼ cup (30g) cacao nibs

¼ cup (20g) coconut flakes or chips

¼ cup (25g) dried blueberries

¼ tsp Himalayan rock salt

1. Combine the ingredients in a medium bowl and mix well.

2. Enjoy as a pick-me-up, snack or dessert.

TIP: You can make all sorts of nut-free mixes using ingredients like goji berries, dried fruit (check for added sugar), spices and seasonings like tamari or salt blends.

INGREDIENT SPOTLIGHT

Cacao nibs are small chunks of cacao beans that have been cultivated in South America and Mexico for thousands of years. Cacao beans have been used as a currency in some cultures – the Aztecs even believed them to be of divine origin! Cacao is a form of chocolate that has not been combined with sugar, milk solids and other industrial ingredients, and is full of nutrients. It is one of the best sources of Magnesium, which balances brain chemistry, builds strong bones, and helps regulate heartbeat and blood pressure. Magnesium is also believed to play a role in preventing muscle cramps and improved recovery for active people.

SALADS
AND SIDES

Beef bone broth
Sweet potato salad
Primal party platter
Maple roasted carrots
Cabbage, coriander and carrot salad with sesame vinaigrette
Lemon and garlic green beans
Toasted seeds
Pickled radishes
Classic herb roast vegetables
Cauliflower 3 ways
Spicy pumpkin and coconut soup
Baby potatoes with flowering chives
Tuna Nicoise salad

Beef Bone Broth

The healing power of gelatine and collagen found in broths is very underestimated. Gelatine supports healthy skin, nails and hair, promotes probiotic balance and growth and is used as a treatment for joint pain and function. Both gelatine and collagen are associated with protection and soothing of the gut lining and may prove useful for leaky gut syndrome and the autoimmune disorders that accompany it.

1kg (2.2lb) beef bones from a high quality source (grass-fed/organic)

3-4L (1 gal) filtered water

3 tbsp apple cider vinegar

1 tsp rock salt or sea salt

2 brown onions, peeled and chopped

4 carrots, peeled and diced

2 celery stalks, chopped (you can use the leaves too)

2-3 garlic cloves

Large handful of fresh parsley (10g)

1. Preheat the oven to 180°C/356°F.

2. Line a large baking tray with aluminium foil or baking paper and spread the bones over the tray in one layer. Roast for 30 minutes to brown the bones and improve the flavour.

3. Remove the bones from the oven, place them into a large stock pot and add the filtered water and vinegar. Cover and let sit for 15-20 minutes to allow the vinegar to draw some of the nutrients from the bones before heating.

4. Add all the chopped vegetables and salt, except for the garlic and parsley.

5. Bring the broth to the boil then reduce to a low simmer (as low as you can) for 48 hours.

6. In the first few hours of simmering, check the broth and scrape off any impurities, foam or froth that floats to the top of the pot and discard.

7. In the last 30 minutes, add the parsley and garlic to the pot.

8. Remove from the heat and let cool slightly. Using a fine metal strainer, remove all the bones, vegetables and other debris and pour the broth into recycled jars to store for later use. They will freeze well too!

TIP: Different types of broth require different cooking times. For chicken broth, we recommend simmering for around 24 hours, and for fish broth, 8-10 hours. Broth works a treat in the slow cooker too – you can set it on low in the garage or laundry and leave it to simmer away!

Sweet potato salad

This is a much healthier take on the classic potato salad recipe. By using sweet potato, we're getting access to higher levels of beta-carotene and more nutritional value.

4 cups (1 litre) water

3 large orange sweet potatoes

4 eggs, hard-boiled

¼ cup (60ml) apple cider vinegar

¼ cup (60g) Dijon-style mustard

½ cup (125ml) macadamia nut oil (or extra virgin olive oil)

1 tbsp sesame oil

2 tbsp fresh chives, chopped

Salt and pepper to taste

1. Bring a pot of water to the boil.

2. Peel and chop the sweet potato into bite-sized chunks and add to the water to cook for 10 minutes or until the potato starts to soften. Once cooked, drain and sprinkle with salt and pepper. Let cool.

3. Peel the hard-boiled eggs and cut in half. Remove the yolks, break them up with a fork and set aside. Roughly chop the egg whites.

4. In a large pitcher or mixing bowl make the dressing by combining the vinegar, mustard, salt and pepper, egg whites and egg yolks.

5. Whisk the dressing and slowly add the macadamia nut oil and sesame oil. Continue to whisk until the liquid forms an emulsion (combines together).

6. In a large bowl, fold the dressing and chopped fresh chives through the sweet potato chunks. Be gentle so that it doesn't turn into a mash. Garnish with extra chives.

7. Leave to marinate in the refrigerator for a few hours or overnight.

This is a great salad to bring along to your next barbecue and is always very popular!

Primal party platter

This party platter will satisfy your guests and they won't even realise that it doesn't have crackers and cheese!

1 tsp coconut oil or ghee

1 Spanish chorizo

2 Granny Smith apples, sliced thinly

mixed cherry tomatoes, try to get different colours

6-8 slices (200g/7oz) ham (nitrate free)

½ cup (90g) mixed olives

1 small cucumber, sliced

½ cup (120g) cashew cream (page 49)

½ cup (120g) capsicum and chilli sweet potato dip (page 58)

1. In a hot pan, melt the coconut oil.

2. Slice the chorizo into diagonal pieces and pan-fry until brown and crispy (about 5 minutes). Set aside to cool.

3. Arrange all ingredients on a serving platter and serve with toothpicks. Encourage combos like apple, chorizo and cashew cream or cucumber and dip wrapped in ham!

This platter can be adapted to suit the foods that you have available. Other ideas could include sauerkraut, pineapple, vegetable chips, nuts, veggies sticks and other healthy dips.

Maple roasted carrots

1 bunch of baby carrots with tops intact

3cm (1 tbsp) chunk of fresh ginger, peeled and grated

1½ tbsp ghee, melted

1 tbsp pure maple syrup

1. Preheat the oven to 150°C/300°F.

2. Chop the tops off the baby carrots, leaving about 6cm (2 inches) of the stem. Discard the tops.

3. Place carrots in a baking dish with the ghee, maple syrup and ginger. Mix well.

4. Roast for 10-15 minutes, until the carrots are starting to caramelise. You may need to stir them occasionally to prevent burning.

5. Serve as a sweeter side with roast chicken, steak or on their own.

INGREDIENT SPOTLIGHT

Maple syrup is one of the best sweetener options on a Paleo diet. Maple syrup is a natural product, a sweet sap created by the Maple tree. Compared to sweeteners like agave syrup and high fructose corn syrup, maple syrup has a much lower level of fructose and like raw honey, stevia and molasses, is much less pro-cessed and has been made for hundreds of years. Make sure that you buy a raw, real maple syrup in its natural form.

Cabbage, coriander and carrot salad with sesame vinaigrette

SERVES 4

2 carrots, peeled and grated

½ head red cabbage, sliced finely

1 tbsp sesame seeds

½ cup (10g) fresh coriander leaves

¼ cup (60ml) extra virgin olive oil

1 tbsp lime juice

1 tsp apple cider vinegar

2 tsp sesame oil

1. In a large bowl, toss the grated carrot, cabbage, sesame seeds and coriander.

2. Measure all other ingredients into a glass jar. Screw the lid on tight and shake the jar until the mixture starts to bind together (emulsify).

3. Pour over salad and mix well.

Lemon and garlic green beans

500g/1.1lb green beans, trimmed and washed

1½ tbsp tallow, butter or ghee

2 garlic cloves, crushed

2 tbsp lemon juice

TO SERVE

1 tbsp slivered almonds, crushed

Lemon rind, shaved into thin strips

Chilli salt

1. Half fill a large mixing bowl with ice water.

2. In a medium saucepan, bring 4-5 cups (1-1.25 litres) of water to a rolling boil. Add a pinch of salt.

3. Drop the green beans into the pot and blanch for 2 minutes, until bright green in colour but still crispy.

4. Drain and place into ice water immediately to suspend the cooking. Once cool, remove the beans and drain.

5. In a large frying pan or wok, heat your fat of choice over medium. Add the garlic and stir frequently to prevent burning it.

6. Add the beans and lemon juice and toss to combine. Once mixed, remove from the heat.

7. Top with crushed almonds, lemon rind and chilli salt to serve.

TIP: If you're including a little dairy in your diet, this recipe is delicious with some high quality goat's cheese or feta. You can also top the dish with some toasted seeds (page 79) instead of lemon and almonds for a different texture and flavour.

Toasted seeds

This toasted seed mix adds some healthy fats and crunchy texture to almost any salad. Make a big batch and store in an airtight jar in your pantry. The trick in making this mix is to make sure that the temperature of the pan is kept as low as possible to avoid damaging the unsaturated seed oils.

½ cup (77g) sesame seeds

½ cup (70g) pepitas (pumpkin seeds)

½ cup (70g) sunflower seeds

2 tbsp chia seeds

2 tsp salt flakes

1. Into a large dry pan on *low* heat, add the sunflower seeds and pepitas. Using a wooden spoon or spatula, stir the seeds constantly to make sure they don't burn. Mix well for about 60 seconds.

2. Add the sesame seeds and stir for another minute, or until all seeds are a light toasted brown.

3. Transfer to a bowl and set aside until cool. Add the chia seeds and salt and mix well.

4. Store in a recycled jar in a cool, dark place.

Pickled radishes

1 part white vinegar (½ cup/125ml)

1 part apple cider vinegar (½ cup/125ml)

1 part filtered water (½ cup/125ml)

1 heaped tsp salt

1 heaped tsp honey (or sweetener of choice)

Bunch of radishes, washes and chopped

2 springs fresh thyme

½ tsp peppercorns

½ tsp mustard seeds

1. Combine the vinegar, water, salt and honey and stir until dissolved.

2. In a (approximately 1L/2 pints), place all chopped radishes, thyme, pepper and mustard seeds.

3. Fill the jar with the vinegar mixture. Make sure the preserving liquid fully submerges the radishes and other ingredients (push them down with a clean fork if need be). Cap and place in the fridge.

TIP: The vinegar and salt in this recipe will help to preserve the radishes and they will keep for up to a couple of weeks in the refrigerator. If you want to preserve them for longer, sterilise the jar first.

Classic herb roast vegetables

Particularly in winter, a big batch of roast veggies is a great side for any meat dish or as a real-food option for post training recovery. You can make a big batch of these to have on hand for lunches and high carbohydrate snacks.

½ Kent pumpkin (1.5kg/3.3lb), or other variety

4 small Spanish (red) onions, peeled

4 large sweet potatoes (1.5kg/3.3lb), peeled

3 garlic cloves, peeled

3 tbsp ghee, melted

¼ cup (8g) chopped fresh rosemary

2 tbsp fresh lemon thyme

2 tsp ground salt flakes

1. Preheat the oven to 200°C/390°F. Line a large baking dish with aluminium foil to make clean-up easier.

2. Using a sharp knife, remove most of the pumpkin skin, but not all.

3. Chop the pumpkin, onion and sweet potato into large chunks and place them in the baking dish with the garlic cloves. Drizzle with the ghee and mix well.

4. In a small bowl, combine the salt, rosemary and thyme. Sprinkle over the veggies.

5. Roast for 75 minutes, turning once, or until tender and lightly golden.

A touch of balsamic vinegar can be a great addition to roast veggies as they're cooking and will create and rustic glaze and add a deep red colour to the dish.

Cauliflower three ways

Cauliflower is a super-vegetable. It's jam packed with anti-inflammatory and cancer-fighting properties and is incredibly easy to whip up into a filling base for any meal. Cauliflower is a great way to sneak some veggies into your day or onto the plate of little ones! These are just three of the many ways that you can transform the humble cauliflower in your kitchen.

Cauliflower mash

—— **SERVES 8** ——

3 cups (750ml) water

1 large head of cauliflower, cut into chunks

2 tbsp ghee (or butter)

1 tsp salt

1 tbsp onion powder

1. Add the water to a large pot and bring to the boil.

2. Place the cauliflower chunks in a vegetable steamer and cover with the lid.

3. Steam over the pot of boiling water for 10 minutes or until the cauliflower is soft and cooked through.

4. Drain the cauliflower and add to a large bowl on your food processor, fitted with a standard chopping blade. A hand-held stick blender will work too.

5. Add the ghee, salt and onion powder.

6. Pulse until smooth. You may need to use a spatula to stir the mixture once or twice.

Cauliflower 'rice'

1 large head of cauliflower, cut into chunks

2 tbsp ghee

1 tsp salt

1 tsp ground pepper

1. Put the raw cauliflower in the large bowl fitting of a food processor with a standard chopping blade. If you don't have one, you can finely dice the cauliflower with a sharp knife – it will just take a lot longer!

2. Pulse until the cauliflower pieces resemble rice grains. Be careful not to over-process, larger pieces are better than mush!

3. Heat the ghee in a large fry-pan on high.

4. Add the cauliflower 'rice' and salt and pepper.

5. Stir constantly for about 4 minutes with a wooden spoon as the rice cooks and starts to brown.

This rice alternative can be used in so many ways! Make your own cauliflower fried rice with veggies and egg, or season in the pan with leeks, onion, salt and ghee. You can whip up a spiced version by adding flavours like smoked paprika, chilli and curry powder too! Just like cauliflower, broccoli can be used in the same way for a greener version!

Coconut roasted cauliflower

1 large head of cauliflower

½ cup (125ml) coconut cream

1 tbsp cumin

2 tsp curry powder

1 tsp garlic powder

1 tsp chilli powder (optional)

1 tsp salt

Zest and juice of 1 lime

1. Preheat the oven to 200°C/390°F and line a large tray with baking paper.

2. Chop the cauliflower into large slices of a similar thickness and lay flat on the baking tray.

3. Combine all remaining ingredients in a small bowl.

4. Using a basting brush, coat the top of the cauliflower in the coconut-spice mixture.

5. Roast for 30 minutes. The coconut cream should make a 'crust' on the surface of the cauliflower.

You can create all sorts of vegetable mashes and purees to complement most protein options. Examples include carrot and cauliflower puree, sweet potato mash, eggplant puree and chopped kale.

Spicy pumpkin and coconut soup

1 brown onion, diced

1 fresh red chilli (or 1 tsp chilli flakes)

1cm (1 tbsp) fresh ginger, finely grated

1 tbsp Ras El Hanout (Moroccan spice blend)

1 garlic clove, crushed

1 tbsp coconut oil

900g/2lb pumpkin, skin removed and flesh chopped

4 cups (1 litre) vegetable stock

½ can (200ml/6.8 fl oz) coconut cream (optional)

4-6 kaffir lime leaves, de-stemmed and thinly sliced

1. In a large saucepan over medium heat, fry the onion, chilli, ginger, lime leaves, Moroccan spices and garlic in the coconut oil for 2 minutes or until the onion is soft.

2. Add the pumpkin and stir through for 1 minute.

3. Add the vegetable stock and bring to the boil.

4. Reduce to a simmer and cook for 20 minutes or until pumpkin is soft.

5. Once cooled a little, pulse the soup with a hand-stick mixer or in batches in a blender until smooth and creamy.

6. Return the soup to the pot, add the coconut cream (optional) and stir through until just mixed.

7. Serve topped with chilli flakes and kaffir lime leaves.

If you prefer a lighter soup, omit the coconut cream.

Baby potatoes with flowering chives and sesame-mustard dressing

1kg (2.2 lb) baby potatoes, washed and sliced in half

4 garlic cloves, peeled

2 tbsp ghee or butter, melted

½ cup (20g) fresh flowering chives, chopped

FOR THE DRESSING:

1 tbsp Dijon mustard

¼ cup (60ml) apple cider vinegar

¼ cup (60ml) extra virgin olive oil

1 tsp sesame oil

salt and pepper, to taste

1. Preheat the oven to 200°C/400°F.

2. Place the potatoes into a baking dish with the garlic. Add the melted ghee and stir well to lightly coat everything.

3. Cover the dish with aluminium foil and bake for 40 minutes. Remove the foil; stir well and bake, uncovered, for a final 10-15 minutes until the potatoes are browned and starting to go crispy.

4. Toss the chives and a pinch of salt over the warm potatoes.

5. For the dressing, place all ingredients in a recycled glass jar and seal. Shake well until combined and the oil and vinegar have emulsified. Drizzle over the potatoes, or serve as a dipping sauce.

Tuna Nicoise Salad

The correct ingredients and presentation for an authentic French Nicoise salad are much debated. This version of a tuna Nicoise is all about building blocks for dinner parties, fast meals and pre-made lunches. You can pre-prepare all of the ingredients and then serve as a rainbow platter for a filling and high protein plate. If there's always a back-up can of tuna in your pantry, you can make this salad from whatever vegetables you have in the refrigerator!

1 tbsp red wine vinegar

¼ cup (60ml) cold-pressed olive oil

1 tsp Dijon-style mustard

2 large cans (350g/12oz) of tuna in spring water, drained*

½ Spanish (red) onion, diced

1 small cucumber, sliced

10 cherry tomatoes, halved

4 tbsp sauerkraut or other fermented vegetables

1 red capsicum (pepper), sliced

½ cup (10g) chopped fresh parsley

2 eggs, hard-boiled

*You can also use fresh tuna steaks, just marinade in a little macadamia nut oil for an hour. Heat a large skillet on medium high heat or place on a hot grill. Cook the steaks 2- 3 minutes on each side until cooked through.

1. Add the vinegar, olive oil and mustard into a glass jar with a screw top lid. Shake vigorously until well mixed and emulsified.

2. Arrange all salad ingredients around a large, flat bowl. Top with slices of hard-boiled egg.

3. Pour the vinaigrette over the salad and serve!

FISH, POULTRY AND MEAT

Satay prawn and onion skewers with cabbage, apple and coconut slaw

Shredded spicy chicken

Apricot chicken

Mini Shepherd's pie pots

Chermoula fish tacos

Spiced lamb mince with Baba Ghanoush

Chunky chilli con carne

Ginger chilli chicken

Chicken and kale pesto 'pasta'

Satay prawn and onion skewers with cabbage, apple and coconut slaw

—— SERVES 4 ——

FOR THE SLAW:

¼ small red cabbage (200g/7oz), sliced finely

1 green apple, grated

1 tbsp shredded coconut (or flaked)

½ tbsp lime juice

¼ cup Mama's Mayo (page 66)

FOR THE SKEWERS:

4 small brown onions, peeled

4 tbsp tamari (or coconut aminos for a soy free option)

Juice from 1 lime

1 tbsp fresh ginger, finely grated

3 tbsp macadamia nut oil

30 raw king prawns (1kg/2.2lb), peeled, deveined, tails intact

FOR THE SAUCE:

½ cup (115g) tahini (hulled)

1 tbsp lime juice

1 tsp sesame oil

1 tbsp tamari

Pinch of ground rock or sea salt

1. To make the slaw, combine the cabbage, apple, coconut and lime juice in a bowl. Add the mayo and mix well. Cover and set aside in the fridge.

2. Chop the onions into square chunks.

3. In a non-metallic dish, combine the tamari, lime juice, ginger and macadamia nut oil. Add the prawns and onions and leave to marinade in the fridge for at least 3-4 hours.

4. When ready to cook, remove the prawns from the fridge and allow them to come to room temperature before cooking.

5. Skewer the prawns and onions onto 8 soaked bamboo or metal skewers. Aim for 3-4 prawns on each skewer.

6. Grill the prawn skewers for 2 minutes each side or until prawns are cooked through and golden.

7. Meanwhile, to make the sauce, combine the tahini, lime juice, sesame oil, tamari and salt in a small saucepan. When ready to serve, heat the sauce gently to serve warm.

8. Serve the skewers drizzled with the warm tahini dressing and alongside the slaw.

TIP: If you can't get access to sustainable or in-season prawns, swap them for chicken, beef or another seafood like scallops.

Shredded spicy chicken

— **SERVES 4-6** —

FOR THE CHICKEN

1½ tbsp coconut oil

4 (1.2kg/2.6lb) boneless, skinless chicken breasts

2 cups (500ml) chicken or vegetable broth

FOR THE SEASONING

2 tbsp chili powder

2 tsp cumin

½ tsp onion powder

½ tsp garlic powder or minced garlic

1 tsp dried oregano

1 tsp paprika

2 tsp salt

1 tsp black pepper

1. In a medium sized pot, heat the coconut oil on medium-high. When hot, add the chicken breasts and brown for 1 minute on each side.

2. Pour in the broth and bring to the boil.

3. Place a lid on the pot and reduce the heat to a low simmer. Cook for 45 minutes, or until the chicken easily shreds with a fork. If the liquid reduces too much while cooking, add a little more broth as needed.

4. Remove the chicken from the pan and use two forks to shred the meat.

5. Combine all ingredients to make the seasoning (I like to just shake them up in a jar).

6. Add the chicken to a fresh pan and sprinkle with the desired amount of seasoning. Add 1 tbsp of water and mix until combined and heated through.

7. Serve with DIY Mexican fillings and lettuce leaves. Try avocado, chopped tomatoes, red onion, sliced red cabbage and olives.

TIP: If you prefer to cook the chicken in the oven, you can easily complete step 3 and poach the chicken breasts, covered with foil, for 30 minutes in the oven at 180°C/350°F.

Apricot chicken

Here's a healthy take on this classic one-pot meal. No onion soup packets or sugary apricot syrup, but a whole lot of flavour!

2 tbsp macadamia nut oil

2 brown onions, cut into chunks

3 garlic cloves, crushed

600g (1.3lb) chicken thigh fillets, skin on

800g (1.8lb) canned apricots (sugar and preservative free) or 1kg (2.2lb) of fresh apricots, halved and pitted

1 tbsp Moroccan seasoning (sugar-free)

2 cups (500ml) vegetable or chicken stock

2-3 bay leaves

1 tsp sea salt

1. Preheat the oven to 180°C/350°F.

2. In a large cast iron pot or pan over medium-high heat, add the oil and chopped onions and garlic. Stir to soften.

3. If needed, add a little more oil then throw in the chicken thigh fillets. Brown the chicken for 2 minutes on each side.

4. Meanwhile, add one can of apricots to a blender with the Moroccan seasoning. Whizz until smooth. If you don't have a blender, you can mash the apricots in a bowl with a fork.

5. Once the chicken and onion have browned, add the blended apricots and reduce the heat. Stir the pot well.

6. Add the vegetable stock, bay leaves, second can of apricots and salt to the pot.

7. Place the casserole dish in the oven (with the lid on) or transfer to an ovenproof baking dish and cover with aluminium foil.

8. Bake for 60 minutes covered then remove the lid or foil and return to the oven for another 10 minutes. The chicken should be tender and starting to fall apart.

9. Serve with cauliflower rice (page 84) or on its own.

Mini Shepherd's pie pots

—— SERVES 4-6 ——

3 tbsp ghee

1 brown onion, peeled and diced

3 garlic cloves, crushed

1kg (2.2lb) grass-fed lamb mince

2 medium carrots, peeled and diced

2 cups (500ml) lamb stock

½ cup (125ml) red wine

4 tbsp tomato paste

1 cinnamon quill

½ tsp allspice

1 tsp salt

2 bay leaves

2 tsp arrowroot powder

2 large sweet potatoes, peeled and chopped into small chunks

1. Heat 1 tbsp ghee over medium-high and sauté the onion and garlic until soft and translucent.

2. Add the lamb mince and stir frequently until lightly browned on all sides (about 10 minutes).

3. Add the carrot, stock, wine, tomato paste, spices, salt and bay leaves. Mix well and reduce to a low simmer. Cover and cook for 35 minutes, stirring occasionally.

4. After 35 minutes, add 1tbsp ghee and the arrowroot powder. Mix through for a minute until slightly thickened. Cook for a further few minutes uncovered and turn the heat off.

5. Place sweet potato in a saucepan and cover with water. Bring to the boil and cook for 15-20 minutes until soft.

6. Drain well and mash with 1 tbsp ghee and salt to taste.

7. Heat the oven to 200°C/390°F.

8. Spoon the lamb mixture into the bottom of small ovenproof ramekins, filling them about ¾ full. Spread the mash on top of the lamb to fill the dishes and scrape with a fork to rough up the top.

9. Bake for 10-15 minutes and then place under a hot grill for 5 minutes to toast the top of the potato.

If you don't have small ramekins, use a large baking dish instead.

Chermoula fish tacos

700g (1.5lb) white fish fillets (halibut or similar)

1 Spanish (red) onion, peeled and diced

3 vine ripened tomatoes, diced

1 serving guacamole

1 head of iceberg or butter lettuce

¼ head of red cabbage, finely sliced

2 tbsp coconut oil

CHERMOULA

¼ cup (5g) chopped fresh coriander

¼ cup (5g) chopped fresh parsley

⅓ cup (80ml) macadamia nut oil

2 garlic cloves, chopped

1 whole small red chilli, chopped

Zest of two lemons

¼ cup (60ml) lemon juice

1 tbsp ground cumin

2 tsp ground coriander

2 tsp smoked paprika

1 tsp salt

1. To make the seasoning, add all Chermoula ingredients into a food processor and pulse until a thick paste forms. Add salt and pepper to taste.

2. Lay all fish fillets flat in a non-metallic dish. Baste with half of the Chermoula mixture. Flip each fillet and baste the remaining puree over the fish so that all sides are seasoned. Marinate for at least a couple of hours in the refrigerator.

3. Meanwhile, arrange all the taco fillers on a large serving platter.

4. Wash and separate the iceberg or butter lettuce into large leaves to act as tortillas.

5. Heat a large pan on medium heat. Add the coconut oil and fry the fillets in batches until just cooked through (around 5 minutes).

6. Place the cooked fish in a serving dish and use a knife or spatula to gently flake into smaller pieces.

7. Place all ingredients in the middle of the table for a DIY taco feast!

Make guacamole by mashing the flesh of 2 avocados with 1/2 Spanish (red) onion, finely diced, the juice from 1 lime, 1 tsp each of ground salt and freshly ground pepper, and 1 small red chilli, diced (optional).

Spicy lamb mince with Baba Ghanoush

—— SERVES 4 ——

3 tbsp macadamia nut oil

½ white onion, finely diced or grated

5 garlic cloves, finely chopped

500g (1.1lb) finely grated lamb mince

6 medium tomatoes, chopped

2 tbsp tomato paste

3 tsp sumac

1 tsp paprika

1 tsp dried chilli flakes

2 tbsp flat-leaf parsley, chopped

1. Heat the oil over medium-high in a frying pan.

2. Add the onion and garlic and stir until fragrant and clear (be careful not to burn it!).

3. Add the lamb mince and stir well.

4. Add the chopped tomatoes and tomato paste and reduce the heat slightly. Use a spatula to smash the tomatoes down as they soften.

5. Add the spices and cook over low heat for 20 minutes, until cooked through and tender.

6. Top with chopped parsley and serve with Baba Ghanoush (page 58), cauliflower rice and fresh cucumber slices.

The flavours and spices in this recipe also make a great fritatta! Once cooked, add the mince to a large fry-pan with 8-10 well-mixed eggs, cover and simmer on low for 15-20 minutes, or until the egg is just set.

Chunky chilli con carne

1kg (2lb) grass-fed beef steak, diced (chuck or stew meat)

500g (1lb) grass-fed beef mince

1 tbsp dried oregano

1½ tbsp ground cumin

2-3 tbsp macadamia nut oil

2 white onions, diced

4 garlic cloves, crushed

800g (1.8lb) canned diced plum tomatoes

3 tbsp tomato paste

4-5 tbsp chilli sauce (find one with no sugar or preservatives)

½ tsp cayenne pepper

1 tbsp raw cacao powder

Salt to taste

Fresh cilantro (coriander) and diced Spanish (red) onion to serve

1. In a large mixing bowl coat the diced beef and mince with oregano and ground cumin.

2. In a large cast iron pot, heat the oil over medium-high heat. Add meat and stir for 2 minutes until brown almost all over.

3. Add the diced onions and garlic and stir for another 3 minutes or so until the onion is translucent and fragrant.

4. Add the canned tomatoes, tomato paste, chilli sauce, cayenne pepper and raw cacao. Adjust the amount of chilli to suit your preference.

5. Reduce to a simmer (there should be just enough liquid to cover the meat, but if it's looking dry, add some more tomato paste or a little water).

6. Simmer on low for 3-5 hours until the beef chunks start to break down.

This chilli is delicious on top of a baked sweet potato, folded in lettuce cups, on its own or as a healthy nachos topping! Serve with diced red onions and fresh coriander.

Ginger chilli chicken

—— SERVES 4-6 ——

This is a favourite marinade for chicken but also works well with beef and prawns. It's a great idea to make a big batch and store in the refrigerator for a fast, easy and delicious source of protein.

½ cup (125ml) tamari (wheat-free soy sauce)

1 tsp sesame oil

3cm (1 tbsp) fresh ginger, peeled and finely grated

2 garlic cloves, crushed

Rind of ½ lemon

Juice from ½ lemon

1 small fresh red chilli, finely chopped

2 tbsp sesame seeds

6 chicken drumsticks

1. Measure all marinade ingredients into a non-metallic, ovenproof dish and stir well.

2. Add the chicken drumsticks and flip a few times to coat them. Cover and set in the refrigerator for at least three hours.

3. Before cooking, bring the chicken to room temperature. Preheat the oven to 180°C/350°F.

4. Bake for 30-35 minutes, until browned and cooked through.

5. Serve with a big pile of roast veggies or on top of your favourite salad mix for lunch.

This recipe works really well with chicken thighs too. I like to make a full tray of thighs, allow them to cool and then chop the chicken roughly to create a pre-made protein for salads and fast meals.

Chicken and kale pesto 'pasta'

—— SERVES 2 ——

Zucchini 'noodles' are an amazing Paleo replacement for pasta, which is high on the list of inflammatory foods. This miraculous noodle substitute will inspire you to cut the pasta for good and get creative. This 'pasta' is delicious with meatballs, bolognaise and in salads too.

This is an easy and affordable meal that can be made in a matter of minutes, with some simple planning and meal preparation ahead of time. For a meat free lunch option, just two zucchini and some pre-made pesto is all you need!

4 green zucchinis
(courgettes)

1 tbsp coconut oil or ghee

2 skinless chicken thigh
fillets, quartered

¼ cup (65g) kale and basil
pesto

Handful of spinach leaves
to serve

KALE AND
BASIL PESTO

1 basil plant or large bunch,
large stems removed

¾ cup (175ml) extra virgin
olive oil

3 large kale (Tuscan
cabbage) leaves,
de-stemmed and chopped
(about 1.5 cups/100g)

½ cup (80g) raw cashews

¼ cup (30g) pistachios

1 tbsp chopped mint

Salt, to taste

1. Place all the pesto ingredients in a food processor and pulse until smooth. Scrape the pesto into an airtight jar and keep in the refrigerator.

2. Roughly peel the zucchini and chop off both ends. Using a handheld julienne device or vegetable spiraliser, process the zucchinis into noodle-like pasta, discard the core (or use it in your next green smoothie!).

3. Heat the oil in a pan on medium-high. Add the chicken, turning regularly until browned and cooked through, about 10 minutes.

4. Add the pre-made pesto and stir for 1 minute to coat the chicken.

5. Add the zucchini and stir for another minute. Turn off the heat and dish into bowls immediately to prevent the zucchini from turning soggy.

SWEETER TREATS

Barbecued pineapple skewers

Watermelon and basil granita

Strawberry and coconut ice-cream

Chewy mocha powerballs

Lemon thyme roast peaches with vanilla cashew cream

Mixed berries with lavender cashew cream

Strawberry and green tea icy poles

You will notice that there aren't a large amount of Paleo desserts in this section. Although sweeter treats are a part of life and popular in Paleo cooking sources, I wanted this book to represent a balanced and sugar-free approach to everyday life. Many people who experience a transition into a primal way of living will kick their sugar habit, and therefore not crave as many sweets and treats throughout the day. If we start to introduce Paleo desserts that use a large amount of 'natural' sugars, we can continue to fuel our reward response and fuel an addiction to sugar without realising it. The desserts in this section are mostly based on whole-fruit and crowd-pleasers that you can bring to your next barbecue or make for an after-school treat for your kids. As they contain no hidden, refined or artificial sugars, these sweeter treats are suitable for the occasional morning teas, boosts of energy and fuel for exercise. It might be helpful to have some of these options around the house when you first transition into the Paleo diet, as you may find it harder to kick the sugar habit than you think!

Barbecued pineapple skewers

— SERVES 4 —

2 medium pineapples, peeled with tops removed

8 skewers (preferably metal)

¼ cup (85g) raw honey

Juice from 1 lime (3 tbsp)

Handful of fresh mint leaves, to garnish

1. Remove the middle core of each pineapple and chop the flesh into bite-sized cubes.

2. Thread the pineapple pieces onto the skewers and place in a shallow baking dish.

3. In a small pitcher, mix the honey and lime juice and pour evenly over the skewers. Leave to marinate in the refrigerator for a couple of hours.

4. On a medium heat, barbecue the skewers for 3-5 minutes with the lid closed. When ready, they should be slightly caramelised and soft.

5. Allow to cool then garnish with fresh mint and slices of lime.

Other sweet fruits are delicious caramelised on the BBQ too! Try juicy peaches or apricots.

Watermelon and basil granita

2 cups (300g) frozen, cubed watermelon

½ small red chilli or ½ tsp chilli flakes (optional)

5 basil leaves, plus a few for serving

Lime rind and salt, to serve (optional)

1. In a food processor, pulse all ingredients to slowly break up the frozen watermelon. Over-process and you will end up with fancy watermelon juice!

2. Just as it reaches a sorbet-like consistency, scoop into small bowls and top with some basil sprigs.

At your next trip to the Farmer's market, stock up on cheap, in-season fruit like watermelon or peaches. Peel, dice and freeze in sealed bags or containers for a quick and easy dessert like this.

Strawberry and coconut ice-cream

1 cup (130g) frozen strawberries

1 frozen banana

¼ cup (60ml) coconut cream, chilled in fridge

2 tbsp coconut flakes

1. Place the strawberries, banana and chilled coconut cream in the large bowl of a food processor.

2. Pulse until the fruit is combined and smooth. This may take a little while (it may go crumbly before it becomes smooth). If necessary, add a little more coconut cream to reach an ice-cream consistency.

3. Add the coconut flakes and pulse to mix gently. Serve with fresh strawberry halves and coconut flakes.

TIP: Add a tablespoon of cacao nibs at step 3 for a strawberry choc chip variation!

You can store leftovers (if there are any!) in the freezer for a quick dessert later. The mixture can freeze quite solid, so leave it to soften a little before digging in.

Chewy mocha powerballs

1 cup raw nuts (e.g. a mix of macadamia and cashew, almonds, walnuts or pecans)

8 fresh Medjool dates, pitted

2 tbsp raw cacao powder

3cm (1 tbsp) chunk ginger, finely grated

2 tbsp coconut oil, melted

1 tbsp coconut flakes

1 tsp cinnamon

1 tsp salt

1 tbsp finely ground coffee beans

2 heaping tbsp goji berries

PLUS, FOR DUSTING:

¼ cup (37g) chia seeds

¼ cup (30g) raw cacao powder

1. In a food processor, add the nuts and pulse until roughly ground but still chunky.

2. Add the pitted dates, cacao powder, ginger, coconut oil, coconut flakes, cinnamon, salt, and coffee. Process until the mixture is starting to stick together (about 60 seconds on high).

3. Add the goji berries and pulse for 15 seconds.

4. Pour the dusting chia seeds and cacao onto two plates.

5. Using your hands, roll the mixture into small balls (about 3cm/ 1 inch across).

6. Roll the balls in the toppings to coat the outer surface.

7. Place in a single layer on a flat plate and set in the refrigerator or freezer until eaten.

The coffee in this recipe is added mainly to create a coffee-chocolate flavour, which is intensified when chilled. If serving in the afternoon or evening, omit the coffee to prevent sleepless nights!

Lemon thyme roast peaches with vanilla cashew cream

4 peaches

1 tbsp maple syrup

Small bunch of fresh lemon thyme, plus extra to serve

6 tbsp cashew cream (page 49)

1. Preheat the oven to 220°C/425°F and line a flat tray with baking paper.

2. Slice each peach in half and remove the stones. Place on the baking tray cut-side up, drizzle with maple syrup and sprinkle with lemon thyme.

3. Roast for 20 minutes or until peaches are soft and starting to caramelise. They should still hold their shape.

4. When making the cashew cream add 1 Medjool date and vanilla from one fresh pod into the blender with the cashews.

5. For each serving, top two peach halves with a dollop of cashew cream and a sprinkle of fresh thyme.

You could easily substitute the cashew cream in this recipe for chilled coconut cream.

Mixed berries with lavender cashew cream

¼ cup (20g) goji berries

½ cup (80g) raw cashews, pre-soaked for 8+ hours with 1/4-1/2 tsp culinary lavender

1 fresh Medjool date, pitted

¼ cup (35g) fresh blueberries

¼ cup (35g) fresh raspberries

1. In a coffee grinder, spice grinder or food processor, whizz the goji berries into a fine powder or dust. Set aside.

2. Wash and drain the soaked nuts and remove the lavender. In a powerful blender or food processor, add the cashews and date and pulse into a smooth cream. Set aside in the fridge.

3. Place the mixed berries in two bowls and top with the cashew cream and goji powder. Garnish with additional culinary lavender if desired.

TIP: You can soak your nuts with a range of ingredients to add infused flavour to many dishes. Try chai spice, cinnamon sticks, vanilla or essential oils like peppermint!

For an extra-delicious dessert, melt some extra dark chocolate in a small ceramic bowl and pour over the top of the berries. Set in the freezer for 10 minutes before serving.

Strawberry and green tea icy poles

—— SERVES 6 ——

2 tea bags of high quality green tea

4 cups (1 litre) filtered water (boiled to 80°C/175°F to prevent making the tea bitter)

2 cups (250g) frozen strawberries, plus about 6 berries kept in chunks/halves

1. In a large jug or glass jar, simmer the green tea in the water until it reaches desired strength (around 5 minutes). Remove the tea bags and allow to cool.

2. In a blender or food processor, puree the strawberries with about 2 tbsp of water.

3. Divide the pureed strawberries into the bottom of the Popsicle moulds.

4. Carefully pour in the green tea to top off each mould and drop a whole berry into each one before inserting the handle.

5. Place in the freezer overnight or until frozen solid.

6. Run warm water over the moulds before loosening and removing each popsicle.

Change up the flavours of your pops with different fruit purees and a variety of tea.

About The Author:

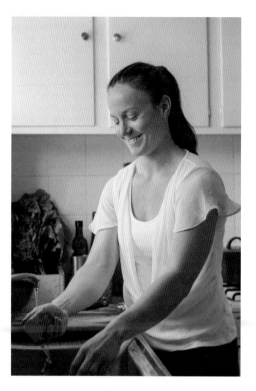

Elizabeth Marsh is a qualified sports scientist and personal trainer from New Zealand. She is currently based in Melbourne, Australia and has worked in the fitness industry for the past 7 years with both recreational and elite level athletes. Through the development of an online and educational community, Primal Junction, her goal is to challenge accepted nutritional and exercise guidelines and encourage individuals to take control of their life through a holistic understanding of real-food, natural human movement, hormonal health, stress reduction and community.

Website: *www.primaljunction.com*

About The Photographer:

Rachel Jane is a self-taught food photographer and stylist based in Melbourne, Australia. As the creator of her beloved blog, Two Loves Studio, she shares her evolving journey into the world of food photography. She is passionate about shooting food portraiture that highlights the simplicity and beauty of real food. Her styling focuses on the shapes and textures of the recipe components, which allows us to connect with the dish and evokes our love affair with food.

Blog: *http://twolovesstudio.com*
Portfolio: *http://racheljane.photography*
Instagram: *http://instagram.com/rjcam*